Handling data

KEY STAGE
ONE

PHOTOCOPIABLES

MATHS HOMEWORK

D0896207

Deleted

impact

Published by Scholastic Publications Ltd,
Villiers House,
Clarendon Avenue,
Leamington Spa,
Warwickshire CV32 5PR

© 1994 Scholastic Publications Ltd
Text © 1994 University of North
London Enterprises Ltd

Reprinted 1994

UNIVERSITY OF
NORTH LONDON

Activities by the IMPACT Project
at the University of North London,
collated and rewritten by Ruth
Merttens and Ros Leather

Editor Jo Saxelby-Jennings
Assistant editor Joanne Boden
Designer Tracey Ramsey
Series designer Anna Oliwa
Illustrations Jane Andrews
Cover illustration Roger Wade Walker

Designed using Aldus Pagemaker
Processed by Salvo Print and Design
Artwork by Pages Bureau,
Leamington Spa
Printed in Great Britain by Clays Ltd,
Bungay, Suffolk

British Library Cataloguing-in-Publication Data
A catalogue record for this book is
available from the British Library.

ISBN 0-590-53159-X

Handling data

impact
C O N T E N T S

Handling data

impact
CONTENTS

impact
INTRODUCTION

This series of IMPACT books is designed to help you run a non-traditional homework scheme. Through the use of take-home maths activities, children can share maths with a parent/carer in the context of the home. The results of these activities then feed back into the classwork at school.

IMPACT works through the following processes:
● Teachers plan their maths for the next few weeks as usual and consider which parts might usefully be done at home.
● Teachers look through selected activities which fit in with what they are planning.
● The activities are photocopied and sent home with the children every week or fortnight.
● The results of each activity are brought back into the classroom by the children and form part of the following week's classwork.

In practice this process will be slightly different in each classroom and in each school. Teachers may adapt it to fit their own way of working and the ethos of the school. Most schools send out IMPACT activities fortnightly, although some do send it weekly. There is some evidence to suggest that weekly activities get a slightly better response and help to raise

standards more effectively than fortnightly, but this is not conclusive. The important point is that each teacher should feel comfortable with how often the IMPACT activities are used in his/her class.

Planning

When you, the teacher, are looking at your work and deciding what maths, roughly speaking, you plan to be doing over the next few weeks, all that is necessary is to consider which parts may usefully be done or practised at home. It is helpful if, over a period of time, a variety of activities are chosen. These tend to fall into three broad categories:
● Activities which practise a skill – these are useful in that they can be followed up in the routine classwork the children are doing. They must be carefully selected by the teacher according to the level of the children.
● Activities which collect data – these lead into work on data-handling and representation.
● Activities in which children measure or make something – this produces an object or some measurements to be used later in class.

The activities in this book are divided into three sections according to age: Reception, Year 1 and Year 2. There are two pages of teachers' notes relating to the individual activities at the beginning of each section. Links to National Curriculum attainment targets are included in the teachers' notes and numerals in brackets refer to the programmes of study, so AT 2/1 (iii, iv) refers to Attainment Target 2, Level 1, Programmes of Study 3 and 4. Details of how these relate to the curricula in Scotland and Northern Ireland are given on page 128.

Working with parents

It is important for the success of IMPACT that the activities taken home are seen by the parents to be maths. We always suggest, at least until IMPACT is up and running and parents' confidence in it is well established, that activities are chosen which have a clearly mathematical purpose. Save the more 'wacky' activities until later! You will get a much better response if parents believe that what they are doing is maths.

Each activity contains a note to parents which explains the purpose of the activity and how they can best help. It also gives a reference to National Curriculum attainment targets – although not to any level. Teachers who prefer not to have these can white them out. The IMPACT activities should be accompanied by an IMPACT diary, enabling parents and children to make their comments. See page 128 for details.

Making the most of IMPACT

The quickest way to reduce the number of children who share the maths at home is to ignore or be negative about the work they bring back into school. When the children come running into the classroom, tripping over the string which went twice round their cat, it is difficult to welcome them all individually but it is crucial that the activities done at home are followed up in classwork. The nature and type of this follow-up work depends very much upon the nature of the activity, and specific suggestions are made in the teachers' notes. However, some general points apply:
● Number activities, such as games, can often be repeated in a more formalised way in the classwork. For example, if the children have been playing a dice game, throwing two dice and adding the totals,

they can continue to do this in the classroom, but this time they can record all the 'sums' in their maths book. This applies to any skills-practice activity.
● Data-collecting activities, of any description, need to be followed up by allowing the children to work together in small groups to collate, analyse and represent their joint data. This will inevitably involve children in a discussion as to how their data was obtained, and any problems they encountered while obtaining it.
● If the children have made or measured something at home, the information or the object needs to be used as part of the classwork. This will not be too difficult since this type of activity is selected by the teacher precisely in order to provide the measurements or shapes for use in class.

The implication of this is that it is wise to select a variety of activities to send home. No teacher wants to drown in data, nor do they want all the IMPACT activities to result in more routine number work. Some activities generate lots of follow-up work while others simply require minimal follow-up – perhaps just a discussion about who won and who lost, and how many times people played the game.

Many of the activities can lead to an attractive display or enable the teacher to make a class book. Such a book does not have to be 'grand'. It can be simply five or six large sheets of sugar paper folded in the middle and stitched/stapled with the children's work mounted inside it. The children love these books, and they make a fine record of their work. An IMPACT display board in the school entrance hall gives parents a sense that their work at home is appreciated.

For further details of IMPACT see page 128.

Teachers' Notes
R E C E P T I O N

Dress the teddies The teddies could be displayed in colour sets. Which is the largest and which is the smallest set? The teddies could then be arranged in a pictogram. Can the children arrange their teddies in a colour pattern that repeats itself which could be displayed on a 'washing line'?
National Curriculum: AT 1/1 (i, ii, iii); AT 2/1 (i, ii); AT 3/1 (i); AT 5/1 (i, ii)

Lay the table The children's work could be displayed around a big picture showing the Three Bears' breakfast table. Which table displayed has the most and which the least family members? Which table shape is the most popular? The children could investigate seating 12 teddies around circular, rectangular, square and triangular tables.
National Curriculum: AT 1/1 (i); AT 5/1 (i, ii)

Find a button The children could work in small groups to devise ways of sorting their buttons. Each group could then try and decide what criteria were used by other groups. The children could display their sets. Are there any overlapping sets? How many criteria were used to classify the buttons?
National Curriculum: AT 1/1 (i, ii, iii); AT 5/1 (i)

Sorting socks The pairs of socks could be sorted into larger groups, for example short or long socks. These could be displayed using different criteria on a 'washing line' and questions asked such as 'Are there more red pairs of socks than blue pairs?' or 'If there are six socks, how many pairs do

we have?' Encourage the children to count in twos, whispering the odd numbers and saying the even numbers. This activity will also help the children to differentiate between odd and even numbers.
National Curriculum: AT 1/1 (i, ii, iii); AT 5/1 (i)

Please may I have a hat? The children could use other hats for sorting, using their chosen criteria. Others could try and guess what criteria had been used. Hats could be displayed in a 'hat shop'. The shop could be used by the children for various money and number activities.
National Curriculum: AT 1/1 (i, ii, iii); AT 5/1 (i)

Animal homes A big wall picture of the mapping exercise could be made illustrating animals and their homes. The children could stick their home activities into a class book to share. Encourage them to investigate wild animals and their homes and produce a large mapping picture.
National Curriculum: AT 1/1 (i, ii); AT 5/1 (iii)

Shoes The children may like to design a chart to show the types of shoes they wear in different weather conditions. These could be drawn and displayed in a mapping picture, using Venn diagrams or a pictogram, and various questions asked as to the style and popularity of the different types of shoes.
National Curriculum: AT 1/1 (i, ii, iii); AT 5/1 (i, ii)

Design a pair of gloves The gloves could be turned over and the children encouraged to play matching games. Hang the gloves on a 'washing line' and practise counting in twos. As an aid to this difficult skill, encourage the children to whisper the odd numbers and speak the even numbers.
National Curriculum: AT 1/1 (i, ii, iii); AT 5/1 (i)

Mapping shoe fastenings Groups of children could sort their school shoes into a variety of different sets: materials, colour, sizes, fastenings and so on, which could be

displayed in a variety of ways. The different methods of fastening could be analysed for their relative advantages.
National Curriculum: AT 1/1 (i, ii, iii); AT 5/1 (i, iii)

Two leaves The children can sit in a circle with at least eight of the leaves in the middle. All the children except one turn round while the one child describes a leaf using three sentences. The rest of the children turn back and try to guess which leaf was being described. The children can sort and stick their leaves into a class book. The comments made will help the children to develop observational skills.
National Curriculum: AT 1/1 (i, ii, iii); AT 5/1 (i)

Toy sorting The children could make a large wall mapping picture illustrating their favourite toys and chosen categories. Questions could be asked, such as, 'Which are the most and least popular categories for the class? Which is the most popular toy? How many children have this toy? Were some toys difficult to categorise? Why?'
National Curriculum: AT 1/1 (i, ii, iii); AT 5/1 (iii)

The lid game The children could stick the lids on to a sheet of paper and map them to particular criteria (such as materials, colours or type of lid). They could be asked questions, for example, 'Which is the most popular colour lid?' or 'How many more red lids are there than blue lids?' The children could then draw pictures of the lids and arrange them as a pictogram. Do they think that it is easier to read the information from a map or from a pictogram?
National Curriculum: AT 1/1 (i, ii, iii); AT 5/1 (i)

Your favourite outfit Tell the children to sit in groups according to the order in which they have drawn their clothes. How many different orders were there? Were some of the orders the children suggested at home impossible to implement? If so, why? The

children could then discuss why some orders are better than others (for example, speed and ease of dressing).
National Curriculum: AT 1/1 (i, ii, iii); AT 5/1 (i)

Cylinder fill The children can sit in a circle in number order to play a game. For example: 'If you have more than 20 objects stand up, if you have more than five but less than ten kneel down.' The children could also sort their objects using different criteria, for example 'made of metal' and 'not made of metal'.
National Curriculum: AT 1/1 (i, ii, iii); AT 2/1 (i, ii, iv); AT 5/1 (i, ii, iii)

Box investigation Let the children construct a collection of cuboids using Polydron. These could be sorted into different sets; for example cuboids with six rectangular faces, cuboids with four rectangular faces, cuboids with two square faces and so on. These could be displayed with other boxes that fit into the same sets.
National Curriculum: AT 1/1 (i, ii, iii); AT 4/1 (i, ii); AT 5/1 (i, ii)

Bags Children can test their bags to see if they work. The bags could be sorted into those made from different materials or with different handle positions. Use the bags to make a 'bag shop'. The shop could then be used by groups of children for money activities.
National Curriculum: AT 1/1 (i, ii, iii); AT 5/1 (i)

Crisp flavours The children could use the crisp packets for a graph of personal preferences. How many of the children's charts have the same preferences as the class chart? Which flavours seemed to be liked best by adults/children, girls/boys and so on. The children's charts could be pinned round the class chart.
National Curriculum: AT 1/1 (i, ii, iii); 2/1 (i, ii, iii, iv); 5/1 (iii, iv)

Frequency of letters The children could use their information and expand it to order all the letters of the alphabet into frequency of use. Each child could draw a bar chart to show the frequency of use of their most popular letters. The children could compare

their results and arrive at a consensus as to the popularity of various letters.
National Curriculum: AT 1/1 (i, ii, iii); AT 1/2 (i, iv); AT 2/2 (ii); AT 5/1 (i, ii)

What shapes are your windows? The children may like to design stained-glass windows using geometric shapes and tissue paper. These designs could then be displayed on a window and the number of different shapes of coloured tissue counted and written undeneath, such as '4 square shapes'. Ask the children which window has the most and which the least square shapes.
National Curriculum: AT 1/1 (i, ii, iii); AT 4/1 (i, ii); AT 5/1 (i)

Which room has the most window panes? The children could sort their windows into different shapes or by the number of panes. For example, how many windows have three panes and are all the panes the same shape? They could investigate how squares and rectangles tessellate and design windows with, say, three shapes, for example one square and two rectangles.
National Curriculum: AT 1/1 (i, ii, iii); AT 4/1 (i, ii); AT 5/1 (i)

Weather The children could work in small groups to show their findings. The activity could be extended in school to map other characteristics of the weather, such as the wind, temperature or sky colour. The results could be displayed, and the symbols for the weather compared with those on television and in newspapers.
National Curriculum: AT 1/2 (i, ii); AT 5/1 (iii)

Windy days The children could make pictograms with the information they bring into school. They could extend the idea on to a calendar for a whole month and then collect the data. Investigate making wind measuring instruments which could be tested for efficiency and a chart kept to record wind conditions.
National Curriculum: AT 1/2 (i, ii); AT 5/1 (iii)

Birthday survey The children could present their information in a different way, such as

using a pictogram, and discuss the relative advantages and disadvantages of their chosen techniques. Their different methods of categorising the information could be displayed and you could ask questions uch as, 'How many people have an autumn birthday?'
National Curriculum: AT 1/2 (i, ii); AT 2/2 (ii, viii); AT 5/2 (i, iii)

How many teddies will fit on to a quarter metre square? The children could make their teddy shape in paper and cut out the number required to cover a quarter metre square. These could be arranged in order as a pictogram with the children's work. If six teddies cover a quarter metre square, how many will cover a metre square? The children could make a metre square and try out their predictions.
National Curriculum: AT 1/2 (i, ii, iii); AT 2/2 (i, viii); AT 5/2 (i, iii)

How many daisies in a metre square? The children could arrange their squares in order of the number of daisies they counted. They could be arranged on a number line with questions, such as, 'How many squares have less than 20 daisies? How many pairs of daisy totals add up to more than 50? How many pairs of daisy totals add up to less than 50?'
National Curriculum: AT 1/2 (i, ii, iii); AT 2/2 (i, viii); AT 5/2 (ii, iii)

Yes! No! The children can play this game in pairs in class. What happens if they have eight cards or ten? Are they any less likely to turn over a 'Yes' first time? Discuss, in general terms, the probabilities if you play with only two cards.
National Curriculum: AT 1/1 (i); AT 5/1 (iv)

Teddy landings Let the children work in groups of four or five and record all their throws. How many times in all did teddy land on the tea towel? How many times did he miss? Talk about the factors that make a difference. For example, does it make any difference how big the teddy bear is?

What about skilled throwing? You can also point out the number bonds to 12.
National Curriculum: AT 2/1 (ii); AT 2/2 (i); AT 5/1 (iv)

What's the chance? Let the children work in groups of two or three and combine their sets. How many things do they have in each set now? Is it hard to think of impossible things? What about certain things? Make a class book of each type of event.
National Curriculum: AT 1/1 (i, ii); AT 5/1 (iv)

Tomorrow The children can collate their information and pictures into large sets labelled 'Likely to happen tomorrow', 'Unlikely to happen tomorrow' and so on. Make a class book of all their pictures, displayed under each of these headings.
National Curriculum: AT 1/1 (i, ii); AT 5/1 (iv)

Animal spinner The children can share their spinners. Make a large class spinner for display with 12 of the best animals drawn on to it. Discuss what the children's chances of getting their animal would be if they spun the twelve spinner. Would it be better or worse than the spinner with only four animals?
National Curriculum: AT 1/1 (ii); AT 5/2 (v)

Night and day The children can share their ideas and then make one large class display with the best of their ideas on it. The night set can be mounted on black paper and the day set on pale blue. In order to make sure that they realise that these sets are the things which are *unlikely* to happen you could mount the sets upside down!
National Curriculum: AT 1/1 (ii); AT 5/1 (iv)

Red and green Working in groups, the children can make a giant 'spinner' for display purposes. They can count up between them the number of times that it landed on red and the number of times that it landed on green. Count up the total number of spins. Collate all the information on to one huge class spinner. This *should* then come out at about half-and-half – that is, even chances of landing green or red.
National Curriculum: AT 1/2 (ii); AT 5/2 (v)

Red and black The children can play this game in pairs in class. What happens if they have a small pack of cards with only ten reds and ten blacks? Does this affect how easy it is to be right? Discuss this. To increase the arithmetic practice they can score the value of the card. The first person to reach a score of 25 is then the winner.
National Curriculum: AT 1/2 (ii); AT 5/2 (v)

Spinner track The children can play this game again in class in pairs and record their spins. How many reds do they spin altogether? How many greens? If you collect up all the class data, does it come out at about half-and-half? Talk about even chances.
National Curriculum: AT 1/2 (ii); AT 5/2 (v)

The good and the bad The children could make a class book or display of their work, collecting together all their good certainties, bad certainties and so on. How many are there in each set? Which set has the most? Can the children think of some likely and some unlikely events? Talk about these.
National Curriculum: AT 1/1 (ii); AT 5/1 (iv)

Upside-down teddy When the children bring in their scores, discuss what were the likely positions for the teddies to land. What were unlikely positions? Why were the scores different for different positions? Are any positions impossible? Can they throw teddy so that he is *certain* to land on his back?
National Curriculum: AT 1/1 (ii); AT 2/1 (vi); AT 5/2 (v)

Kitchen chances Play this game in class using coloured bricks and an opaque bag. If there are more red bricks, for example, do the children understand that they are more likely to take one out? Record which bricks are taken out by colouring in squares on a piece of paper. Does this help them with their subsequent guesses?
National Curriculum: AT 1/1 (ii); AT 2/1 (i, ii); AT 5/1 (iv)

Dress the teddies

YOU WILL NEED: four different
coloured crayons, a pair of scissors,
some adhesive or sticky tape and
another piece of paper.

● Colour the teddies and their clothes
on these two pages. Make sure that
each teddy has a set of clothes that
match (for example, all red or all blue).

● Cut out the clothes and the teddies
and stick the clothes on to the teddies.

● On another piece of paper, draw a
bench and stick the teddies on in a row.

_____and

child

_____

helper(s)

_____

did this activity together

Dress the teddies

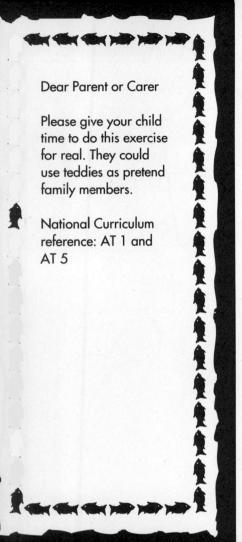

_____and

child

_____

helper(s)

_____

did this activity together

Lay the table

● Draw your family's dining table. Make sure that it is the right shape.

● Draw on the right cutlery and crockery for everyone for dinner.

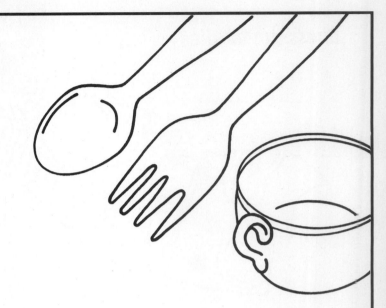

Find a button

● Try to look at a selection of buttons.

● Choose one carefully.
Stick your button in this circle:

● Ask someone at home to help you to write three things to describe your button.

1

2

3

● Please bring your button and descriptions to school.

Dear Parent or Carer

We shall be sorting the buttons in school. Sorting involves choosing criteria. Through this activity your child will have three ideas that you have talked about, such as shape, texture or finish.

National Curriculum reference: AT 1 and AT 5

_____and

child

_____

helper(s)

_____

did this activity together

_____and

child

_____

helper(s)

_____

did this activity together

Sorting socks

● Can you sort all the family socks into pairs?

● Draw round your favourite pair of socks and bring your drawing into school.

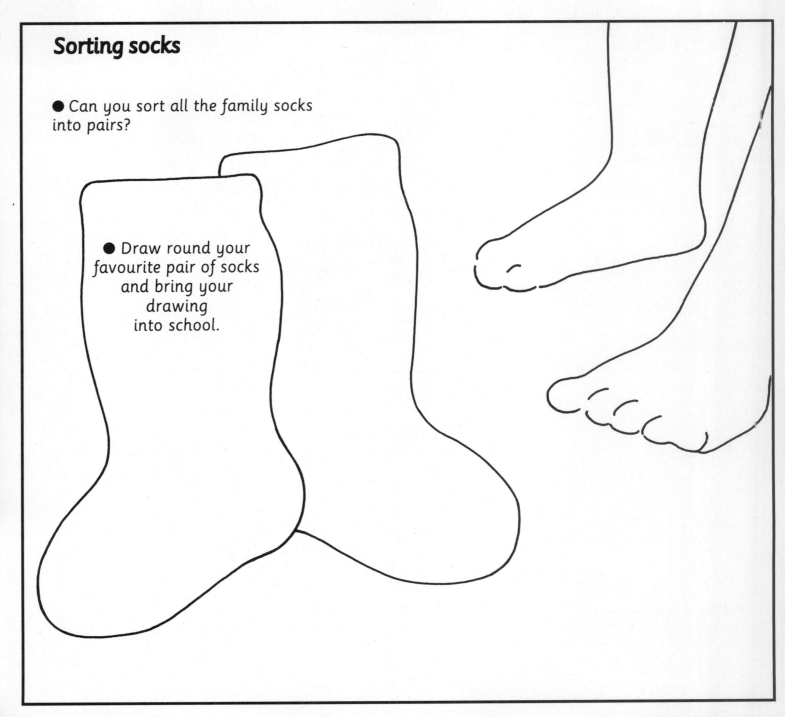

impact MATHS HOMEWORK

Please may I have a hat?

● Find a hat which you can bring to school.

● Write down two things to describe your hat:

1

2

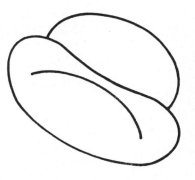

Dear Parent or Carer

Please help your child to choose and then to describe their hat and to write the description down. You could discuss the materials that it is made from, its colour, purpose and so on.

National Curriculum reference: AT 1 and AT 5

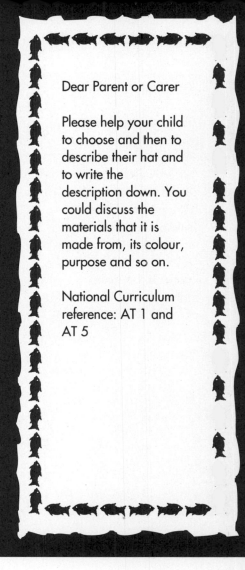

_____and

child

_____

helper(s)

_____

did this activity together

impact MATHS HOMEWORK

_____and
child

_____
helper(s)

_____
did this activity together

Animal homes

● Which animals belong in which homes?

● Can you draw lines to map each animal on to its right home?

● How many animals are there? How many homes?

fish

bird

cat

hamster

rabbit

dog

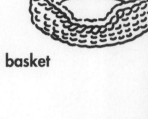

basket

kennel

aquarium

cage

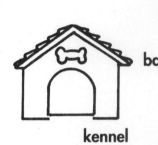

cage

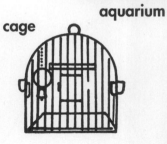

hutch

Shoes

● Find as many different types of shoe as possible.

● Try and sort them into different categories.

● Design a chart to show your favourite sorting. Start below and use the back of this sheet if you need more room.

Dear Parent or Carer

Please help your child to find the shoes and then to think of different ways of sorting them, for example by colour or material.

National Curriculum reference: AT 1 and AT 5

_____and

child

_____

helper(s)

_____

did this activity together

_____and

child

_____

helper(s)

_____

did this activity together

Design a pair of gloves

● Design and colour in a pattern for these gloves.

● Make sure that your gloves match.

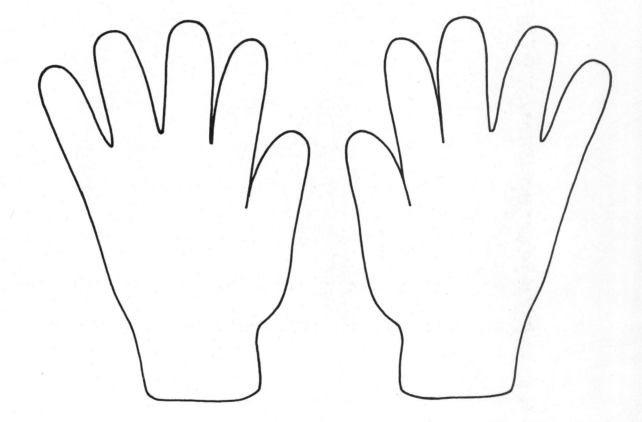

● Please bring them to school.

Mapping shoe fastenings

Laces:

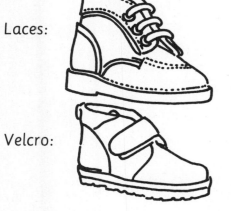

Velcro:

Buckles:

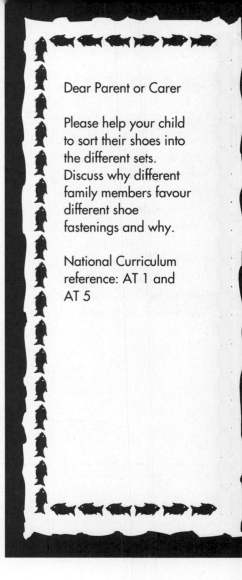

Others:

● List your family members:

● Ask each member of your family to draw a line to his or her name to show how their favourite pairs of shoes fasten.

Dear Parent or Carer

Please help your child to sort their shoes into the different sets. Discuss why different family members favour different shoe fastenings and why.

National Curriculum reference: AT 1 and AT 5

_____and

child

_____

helper(s)

_____

did this activity together

_____and

child

_____

helper(s)

_____

did this activity together

Two leaves

● Find two different leaves.
● Carefully draw round and colour in your two leaves.
● Ask someone at home to help you write three things which are the same about your leaves.

1

2

3

● Now write three things which are different about your leaves.

1

2

3

● Please bring your leaves to school. Flatten them, if you can.

impact MATHS HOMEWORK

Toy sorting

● Please make drawings of some of your favourite toys.

● Draw a line from each picture to the word that describes that toy best.

cuddly

construction

game

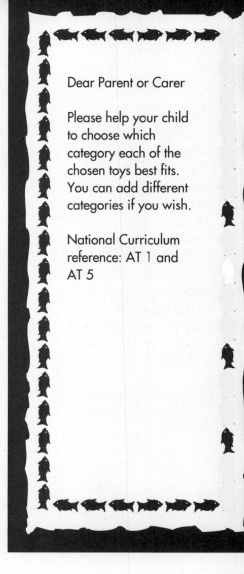

Dear Parent or Carer

Please help your child to choose which category each of the chosen toys best fits. You can add different categories if you wish.

National Curriculum reference: AT 1 and AT 5

_____and

child

_____

helper(s)

_____

did this activity together

_____and

child

_____

helper(s)

_____

did this activity together

The lid game

YOU WILL NEED: at least five different lids or tops to play this game for two people.

● Put the lids in the middle and look at them carefully.

● One person should turn round while the other person describes one of the lids.

● The first person should then turn back round and try to pick out the right lid from the description. Keep the lid if you guess correctly.

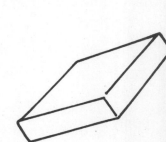
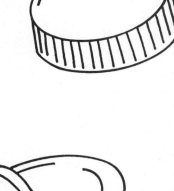
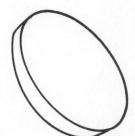

● Take turns, the winner is the one who has the most lids.

● Please bring one of your lids to school.

Your favourite outfit

● Draw your favourite outfit.

● Remember to draw every item that you would be wearing. Draw them in the order in which you would get dressed.

Dear Parent or Carer

Please help your child by allowing them to lay out the clothes that they have chosen in order. You can then check them for omissions and order before your child draws them.

National Curriculum reference: AT 1 and AT 5

_____and

child

_____

helper(s)

_____

did this activity together

_____and

child

_____

helper(s)

_____

did this activity together

Cylinder fill

YOU WILL NEED: an empty toilet roll tube.

● Seal one end of the toilet roll tube.

● How many small things can you fit inside?

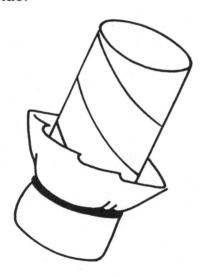

● Please seal the top, and then write your name and the number of articles contained in your cylinder on the outside.

● Bring it to school.

Box investigation

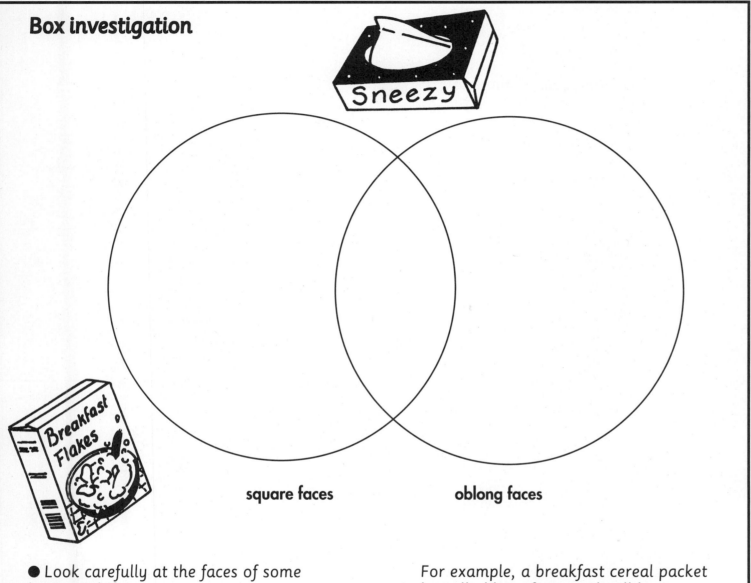

square faces   oblong faces

● Look carefully at the faces of some boxes. Ask first!

● Write the names on the boxes in the appropriate sets.

For example, a breakfast cereal packet has all oblong faces and will be a member of the oblong set.

Dear Parent or Carer

Please talk to your child about the shapes of the faces (sides) that make up boxes:
• all squares = cubes;
• all oblongs = cuboids;
• oblongs and squares = cuboids.

National Curriculum reference: AT 1, AT 4 and AT 5

_____and

child

_____

helper(s)

_____

did this activity together

_____and

child

_____

helper(s)

_____

did this activity together

Bags

● *Use anything you like at home to make a bag large enough to carry a bag of flour.*

● Bring your finished bag into school.

Crisp flavours

● List all the members of your family in the space below.

Members of my family

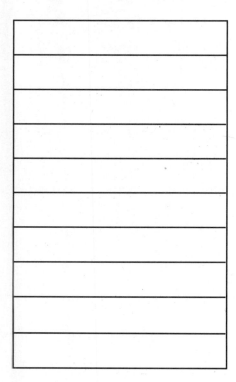

Flavours of crisps

salt and vinegar

ready salted

smoky bacon

cheese and onion

prawn cocktail

beef and mustard

chicken

tomato sauce

Worcestershire sauce

● Draw lines from the names of each of your family members to their two favourite flavours of crisps. Add any extra favourite flavours if you need to.

● Please bring any empty crisp packets to school with your chart.

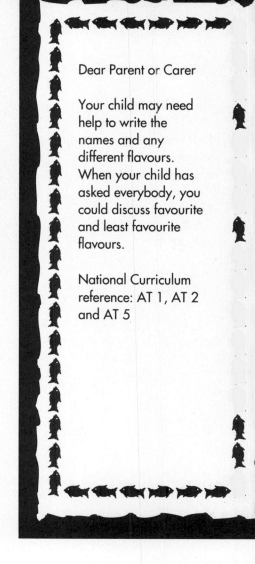

Dear Parent or Carer

Your child may need help to write the names and any different flavours. When your child has asked everybody, you could discuss favourite and least favourite flavours.

National Curriculum reference: AT 1, AT 2 and AT 5

_____and

child

_____

helper(s)

_____

did this activity together

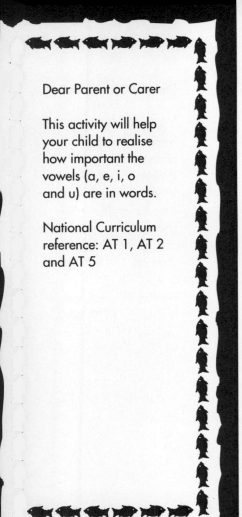
Frequency of letters

● Write down the five letters that you think you will see most often on a page of your reading book:

1

2

3

4

5

● Choose a page in your reading book.

● By each letter opposite make a tally of the number of times it is used on the chosen page.

● Do you want to change any of your letters? Try again:

1

2

3

4

5

What shapes are your windows?

● Draw the windows in your house and make a tally of their shapes.

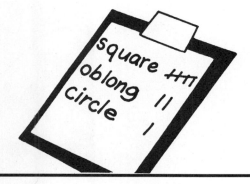

square   ++++ |
oblong ||
circle |

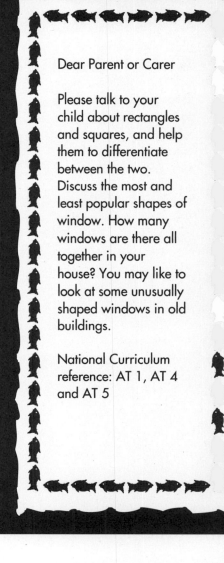

Dear Parent or Carer

Please talk to your child about rectangles and squares, and help them to differentiate between the two. Discuss the most and least popular shapes of window. How many windows are there all together in your house? You may like to look at some unusually shaped windows in old buildings.

National Curriculum reference: AT 1, AT 4 and AT 5

_____and

child

_____

helper(s)

_____

did this activity together

Dear Parent or Carer

Please help your child to choose the right window. Help may also be needed with drawing the shapes.

National Curriculum reference: AT 1, AT 4 and AT 5

_____and

child

_____

helper(s)

_____

did this activity together

Which room has the most window panes?

- Look around your house.

- Draw the window with the most panes.

- Bring your sketch into school.

Weather

● Try and look at the sky at the same time every day for a week.

● Each day draw a line to the symbol that matches the weather.

● Bring your chart to school next week.

I looked at the weather at:

 every day.

Monday

Tuesday

Wednesday

Thursday

Friday

Saturday

Sunday

sunny

cloudy

rainy

_____and

child

_____

helper(s)

_____

did this activity together

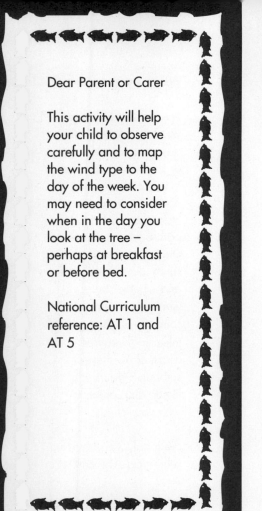

_____ and
child

_____
helper(s)

_____
did this activity together

Windy days

● Every day draw a line to the weather
picture you think is best.

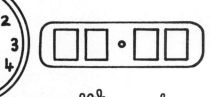

I looked at my tree at: every day.

Monday

Tuesday

Wednesday

Thursday

Friday

Saturday

Sunday

Calm weather –

twigs do not move.

Breezy – twigs and

small branches

move in the wind.

Windy – big

branches move in

the wind.

impact MATHS HOMEWORK

Birthday survey

Ask everyone at home to write their name in the right set.

This year my birthday falls:

on a weekday

in a summer month

in a month with thirty days

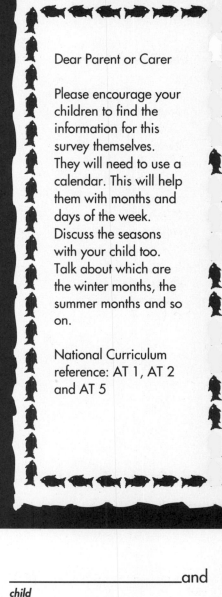

Dear Parent or Carer

Please encourage your children to find the information for this survey themselves. They will need to use a calendar. This will help them with months and days of the week. Discuss the seasons with your child too. Talk about which are the winter months, the summer months and so on.

National Curriculum reference: AT 1, AT 2 and AT 5

_____and

child

_____

helper(s)

_____

did this activity together

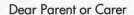

_____and

child

_____

helper(s)

_____

did this activity together

How many teddies will fit on to a quarter metre square?

● Make a square 25cm × 25cm out of newspaper.

● Choose a teddy.

● Try to estimate how many times your teddy will fit on to your square. Lay him down and draw round him as many times as you can.

impact MATHS HOMEWORK

How many daisies in a metre square?

● Make a metre square with strips of paper, card or string.

● Find a suitable place in your garden or local park to put your metre square to count daisies.

● Draw the daisies you counted in this square:

Dear Parent or Carer

Please help your child to cut four 1m length strips of paper, card or string. These can be stuck or tied together or placed under stones to mark the area you have chosen for counting daisies.

National Curriculum reference: AT 1, AT 2 and AT 5

_____and

child

_____

helper(s)

_____

did this activity together

_____and
child

_____
helper(s)

_____

did this activity together

Yes! No!

YOU WILL NEED: six cards cut out from the back of an old birthday or Christmas card.

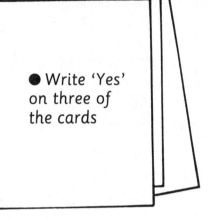

● Write 'Yes' on three of the cards

and 'No' on the other three.

● Shuffle them up and spread them out on the table.

● Take it in turns to turn one card over. You are looking for the 'Yes' cards.

● If you turn over a 'Yes', you can keep it. If you turn over a 'No', turn it back over so that it is face down again. Play until all the 'Yes' cards are taken. Who is the winner?

● Play again. Who wins this time?

impact MATHS HOMEWORK

Teddy landings

YOU WILL NEED: a tea towel, or a piece of newspaper, spread out in the middle of the floor and an old teddy bear.

● Stand a little distance from the tea towel and throw teddy on to it. Does he land on the tea towel?

● Throw teddy 12 times! Ask your partner to record your throws and where he lands. Count as you go.

● How many times does teddy land on the tea towel? How many times does he land off the towel?

● Bring all your results into school.

Dear Parent or Carer

This activity is to help your child to count and also practises his or her knowledge of number bonds to 12. It is part of some work we are doing on the mathematical area of probability.

National Curriculum reference: AT 1, AT 2 and AT 5

_____and

child

_____

helper(s)

_____

did this activity together

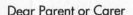

Dear Parent or Carer

This activity is intended to help young children to begin thinking about the mathematical topic of probability, starting by talking about how some events are more likely than others. Later on, we shall talk in terms of mathematical probability.

National Curriculum reference: AT 1 and AT 5

_____and

child

_____

helper(s)

_____

did this activity together

What's the chance?

● Think of some things which can fit in each set.
For example, it is certain that a book will hit the ground if I push it off the table. Or, it is impossible that I will grow another head!

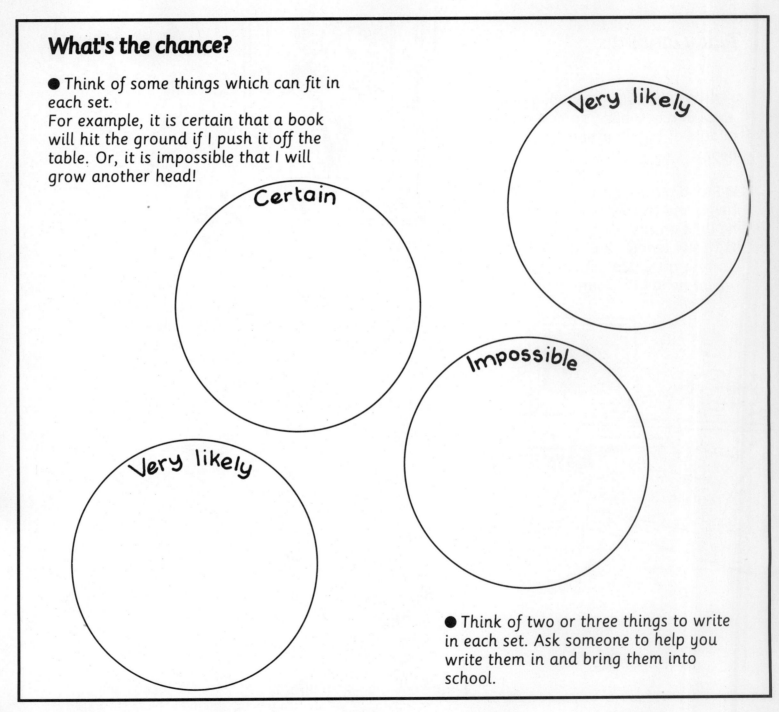

Certain

Very likely

Impossible

Very likely

● Think of two or three things to write in each set. Ask someone to help you write them in and bring them into school.

impact MATHS HOMEWORK

Tomorrow

- What do you think will happen tomorrow?

- Draw a suitable picture in each of the sets below.

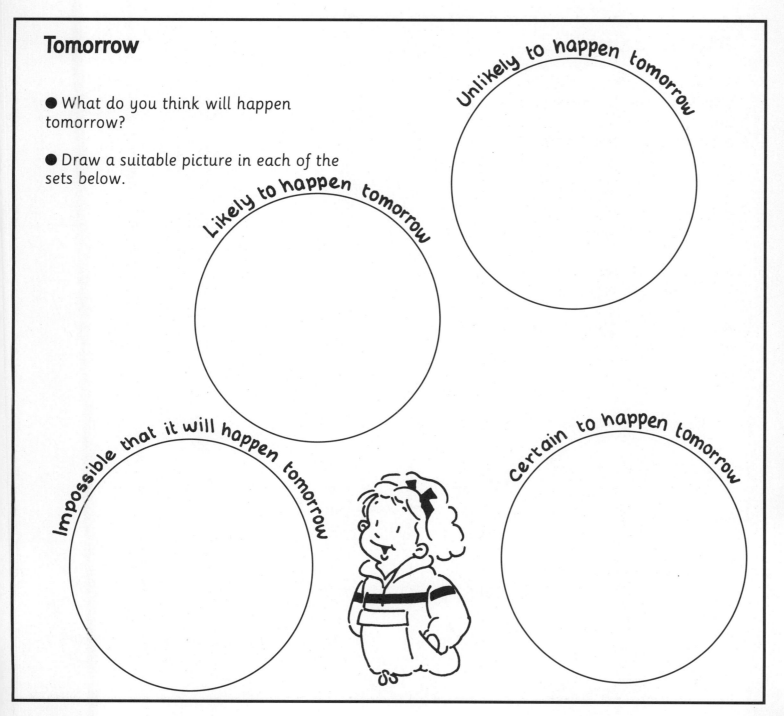

Unlikely to happen tomorrow

Likely to happen tomorrow

Impossible that it will happen tomorrow

Certain to happen tomorrow

Dear Parent or Carer

This activity helps to introduce the idea of 'likelihood' which underpins much of our work in the area of mathematical probability. Discuss your child's predictions with him or her.

National Curriculum reference: AT 1 and AT 5

_____and

child

_____

helper(s)

_____

did this activity together

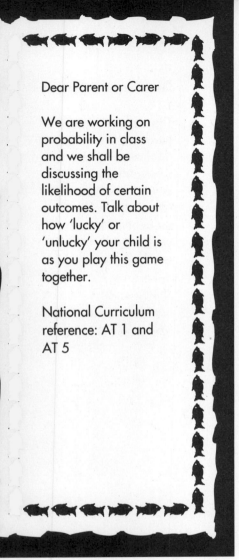
_____and

child

_____

helper(s)

_____

did this activity together

Animal spinner

YOU WILL NEED: an old birthday or Christmas card, a pencil and some counters (raisins will do!).

● Cut out the spinner on this page.

● Stick it on to the back of the old birthday or Christmas card.

● Cut round it and draw a different animal in each segment

● Push a pencil through the middle of your spinner.

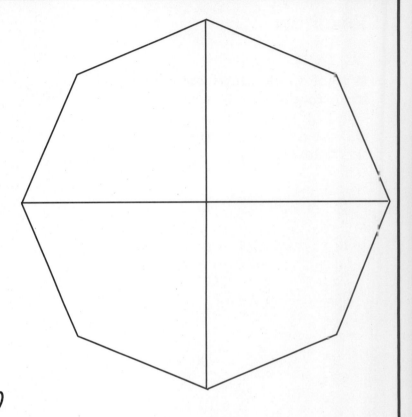

● Decide which animal you are each going to be.

● Take it in turns to spin the spinner. If it lands on 'your' animal, take a counter. If it doesn't, make the noise your animal makes!

● The winner is the first person to get three counters.

impact MATHS HOMEWORK

Night and day

Wouldn't it be surprising if owls flew around in the daytime or robins came out at night?

● Draw three things in the night set which are UNLIKELY to happen in the night!

● Draw three things in the day set which are UNLIKELY to happen in the daytime!

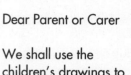

Unlikely at night

Unlikely in the day

● Bring your drawings into school.

Dear Parent or Carer

We shall use the children's drawings to do some work on 'likely' and 'unlikely', which are concepts necessary for understanding the work on probability for which this forms a basis. Talk with your child about what things are *likely* to happen at night and in the day.

National Curriculum reference: AT 1 and AT 5

_____and

child

_____

helper(s)

_____

did this activity together

_____and

child

_____

helper(s)

_____

did this activity together

Red and green

YOU WILL NEED: an old birthday or Christmas card, a red crayon, a green crayon, a pencil and some counters (raisins, coins or small building bricks will do!).

● Cut out the spinner on this page.

● Stick it on to the back of an old birthday or Christmas card.

● Cut round it and colour three of the segments red and three green.

● Push a pencil through the middle of your spinner.

● Each player should choose a colour.

● Take it in turns to spin the spinner. If it lands on your colour, take a counter.

● Have six goes each. Who has the most counters?

● Play again. Does the same person win?

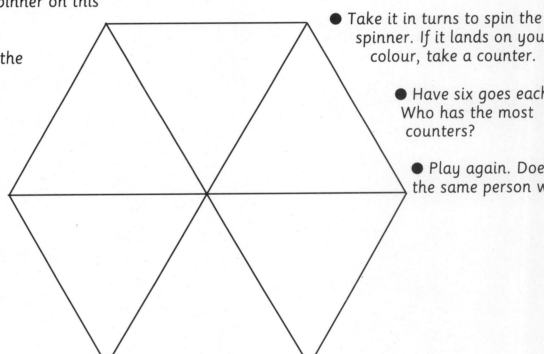

Red and black

YOU WILL NEED: a pack of cards with the face (picture) cards removed.

● Place the pack face down in the centre of the table.

● Guess what colour the top card is going to be.

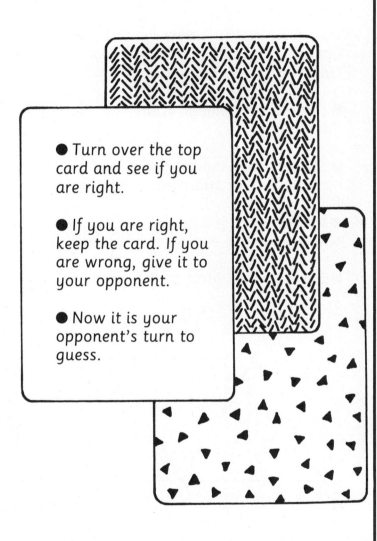

● Turn over the top card and see if you are right.

● If you are right, keep the card. If you are wrong, give it to your opponent.

● Now it is your opponent's turn to guess.

● Play until one of you has ten cards. That person wins!

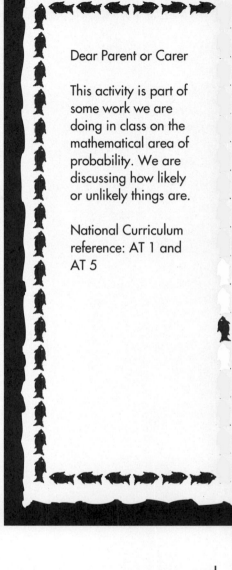

Dear Parent or Carer

This activity is part of some work we are doing in class on the mathematical area of probability. We are discussing how likely or unlikely things are.

National Curriculum reference: AT 1 and AT 5

_____and

child

_____

helper(s)

_____

did this activity together

_____and

child

_____

helper(s)

_____

did this activity together

Spinner track

YOU WILL NEED: an old birthday or Christmas card, a red crayon, a green crayon, a pencil and a counter each.

● Cut out the spinner at the bottom of the page.

● Stick it on to the back of an old birthday or Christmas card.

● Cut round it and colour three of the segments in red and three in green.

● Push a pencil through the middle.

● Also, colour in the track on the accompanying page.

● Choose to be either 'red' or 'green'. One person must be 'red' and the other 'green'.

● Take it in turns to spin the spinner. If you spin a red, move along the track to the next red space if you are 'red' or if you spin a green, move to the next green space if you are 'green'.

● Do not move if you do not spin your colour. If you spin three of the wrong sort in a row, have an extra turn.

● The first person to reach the last space is the winner.

● Play again. Does the same person win? How many extra turns did you each get?

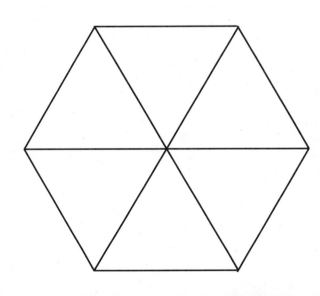

impact MATHS HOMEWORK

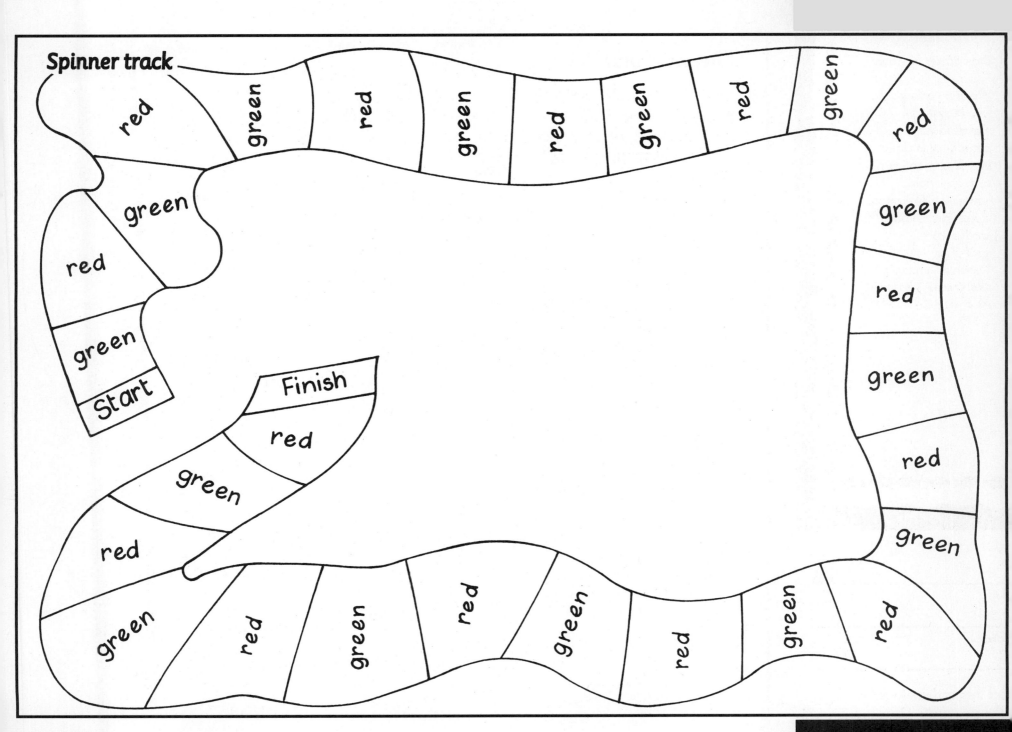

Spinner track

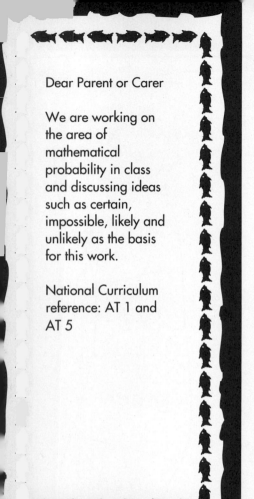
The good and the bad

● Think of at least one good thing and one bad thing which are certain to happen. Draw pictures of them in the right sets.

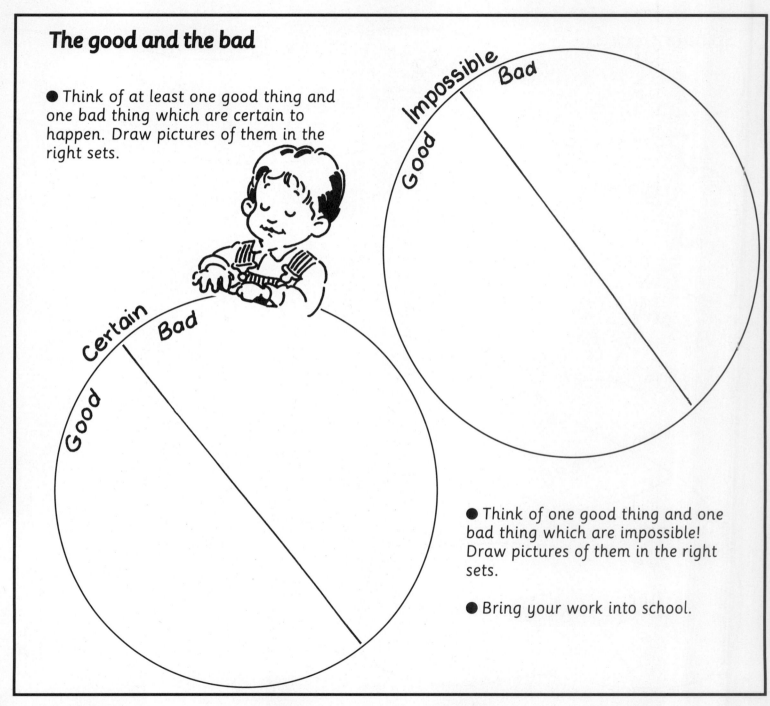

● Think of one good thing and one bad thing which are impossible! Draw pictures of them in the right sets.

● Bring your work into school.

Upside-down teddy

YOU WILL NEED: a teddy bear and some counters (small bricks or buttons will do!).

● Take it in turns to throw teddy up in the air! How does he land?

If he lands on his face – score 1 point.
If he lands on his back – score 2 points.
If he lands in any other position – score 4 points.

● Have five goes each. Who has the most points?

● Play again. Bring all your scores into school.

Dear Parent or Carer

This activity will lead into some work in class on probability. We shall be discussing which events are more likely than others, whether we can predict which are more likely and what the chances are of them happening.

National Curriculum reference: AT 1, AT 2 and AT 5

_____and

child

_____

helper(s)

_____

did this activity together

_____and

child

_____

helper(s)

_____

did this activity together

Kitchen chances

YOU WILL NEED: some forks, big spoons and little spoons and a bag to put them in.

● Count the forks, big spoons and little spoons into the bag. How many of each are there?

● Now shut your eyes and ask your helper to take one out and hide it behind their back. They must take the first one they touch!

● Guess what they have got behind their back; a fork, a big spoon or a little spoon. If you are right, keep it. If you are wrong, it goes on the table.

● Shut your eyes again and ask them to take another and so on.

● Keep guessing. How good are your guesses? How many do you get to keep and how many go on the table?

impact MATHS HOMEWORK

Teachers' Notes
YEAR ONE

Inside out Make number lines divided into five second intervals. The children can cut these into strips to represent their fastest and slowest times from which to find the time differences. Ask them to sit in order. Who took the shortest and who the longest time? Why were some people faster? Is it a fair test?
National Curriculum: AT 1/2 (i, ii, iii); AT 2/2 (viii); AT 5/2 (i, iii, iv)

Lunch-box content The children can discuss which types of food are the most popular. This is an ideal time to discuss healthy eating and tooth care. Make a big chart to illustrate healthy foods and how they are used, for example, calcium for bones and carbohydrates for energy.
National Curriculum: AT 1/2 (i, ii, iii); AT 5/2 (i, ii)

Light search Give the children a set of questions to answer about their activity. For example, how many lights are there all together or how many more ceiling lights are there than table lamps? Display the data and answers in a class book and draw a pictogram drawn of the different types of lights.
National Curriculum: AT 1/2 (i, ii, iii); AT 2/2 (i, iii); AT 5/2 (i)

Brushes The children could stick their drawings of sets into a class book to share. A Venn diagram or a pictogram could illustrate the different criteria. Ask questions such as, 'Did any brush satisfy more than one criteria? Which was the most popular set?'
National Curriculum: AT 1/2 (i, ii, iii); AT 5/2 (i, ii)

More than three buttons Tell the children to bring their results into school. Ask them to guess how each other's articles have been sorted. The children's work could be displayed as a Venn diagram to demonstrate the different criteria chosen. Questions can be asked, such as 'Did any articles appear in more than one set? How was the problem resolved?' (Solution: use intersecting circles.)
National Curriculum: AT 1/2 (i, ii, iii); AT 5/2 (i)

Leaves The children could work in groups and try to use two other criteria to sort the leaves, which could be stuck on to larger rectangles of paper and displayed with their homework around a 'seasons' picture of a horse chestnut tree, for example.
National Curriculum: AT 1/2 (i, ii, iii); AT 5/2 (i, iv)

Wheel tally The children could be encouraged to discuss why their tallies have different results. Perhaps the different locations could be plotted on to a local map. Which are the best locations and why? Are there some times in the day that are better for collecting information than others? Why?
National Curriculum: AT 1/2 (i, ii); AT 5/2 (ii)

How many tins do you open each week? The children could discuss the criteria they have used for grouping their information. Children with the same criteria could produce their own chart to show the results. They could then be encouraged to discuss their findings, such as one group opened eight more pet food tins than drink tins.
National Curriculum: AT 1/2 (ii); AT 2/2 (ii); AT 5/2 (i, ii, iii)

Sorting money The children may like to total the money in each set. Each category could then be ordered in terms of value and differences calculated. The coin rubbings could be displayed in different sets, for example 'up to 15p' and 'over 15p'. Which set contains the most coins?
National Curriculum: AT 1/2 (i, ii, iii); AT 2/2 (iii, v); AT 5/2 (iv)

Street survey The children could tally their information. They may like to put this data on to a street map of their local town. Why do some shops/buildings occur more frequently in some streets than others? How would the children like to improve the facilities of their town? An 'ideal' town could be designed by the class.
National Curriculum: AT 1/2 (i, ii, iii); AT 5/2 (i, ii, iii)

Street furniture Sort the street furniture into different categories, such as informative, for safety and so on. If your children are working in the local environment, this activity will encourage discussion about local improvements and whether all the changes are beneficial.
National Curriculum: AT 1/2 (i, ii, iii); AT 5/2 (i, ii, iii)

Telephone calls The children will need to discuss the different categories they have used. Younger children could record this work as a bar graph or pictogram, older children could enter it on to a computer database. The recording methods can then be interpreted to extract information.
National Curriculum: AT 1/2 (i, ii, iii); AT 2/2 (i, ii, iii); AT 5/3 (i, ii, iii)

Pocket money The children can make charts to show the most popular ways of spending their pocket money. Are there items that they need to save to buy? How much do they save each week? Do girls and boys spend their money on similar or different items?
National Curriculum: AT 1/2 (i, ii, iii); AT 2/2 (iii, v); AT 5/2 (i, ii, iii)

Sorting the grocery shopping Let the children work together in small groups to discuss their methods of sorting and the charts they have devised. Perhaps a class debate could discuss the different methods and their advantages and disadvantages. The children could display the different methods and state why they were chosen.
National Curriculum: AT 1/2 (i, ii, iii); AT 5/2 (i, ii)

Collecting measures Encourage the children to find out why we have different measures for solids and for liquids. They could investigate the weights of various millilitres of water using a 5ml spoon and record their findings.
National Curriculum: AT 1/2 (i, ii, iii); AT 2/2 (viii); AT 5/2 (i)

Word frequency This activity provides an ideal opportunity to look at the frequency of words. The words can be written in large print and displayed around the classroom. Encourage the children to learn to read and write them, knowing that they have a high frequency. Share this information with parents. Emphasise that the children should recognise and remember common words rather than reading them letter by letter every time. For example, 't-h-e' will always be 'the'.
National Curriculum: AT 1/2 (i, ii, iii); AT 2/2 (i, iv); AT 5/2 (i, ii)

Boiling a litre of water The children can design a chart to show their findings and the results analysed. How did the children boil the water? How did they know when the water had boiled? Do electric kettles boil water quicker than kettles or saucepans on a hob?
National Curriculum: AT 1/2 (i, ii, iii); AT 2/2 (viii); 5/2 (ii)

Packing your lunch-box The children could use hour circles demarcated into five minute intervals and colour in the minutes taken to prepare their lunches. Arrange their circles from least to longest time taken. How many took more than 15 or less than ten minutes?
National Curriculum: AT 1/2 (i, ii, iii); AT 2/2 (viii); AT 5/2 (i)

Car registration tally The children could record their work by adding all the individual tallies together. Which year was the most popular? How many cars were older/younger than they are? The results can be displayed as a block graph using a different colour for each year. (They may have to consider using one block to represent more than one car.)
National Curriculum: AT 1/2 (i, ii, iii); AT 2/2 (ii, iv, viii); AT 5/2 (i, ii)

Callers The children could discuss different ways of recording their information, either independently or in groups. Some children could use the computer. Their different methods could be displayed and the advantages and disadvantages discussed and interpreted.
National Curriculum: AT 1/2 (i, ii, iii); AT 2/2 (ii); AT 5/2 (i, ii, iii); AT 5/3 (i, ii, iii)

Less than £1, more than £1 The children could use their information for working with money. Each child could total the two coloured till receipt lists. This information could then be sorted into most and least expensive, totals nearest to £10 and £5 and so on. Differences between most and least expensive could be calculated.
National Curriculum: AT 1/2 (i, ii, iii); AT 2/2 (iii, v); AT 5/2 (i)

Small change survey The children could work in pairs to arrange their days by least to most amount of money. These totals could be made again using the least number of coins possible and recorded. Do large sums of money always take more coins than small sums of money? The children could discuss the reasons for different value coins.
National Curriculum: AT 1/2 (i, ii, iii); AT 2/2 (iii, v); AT 5/2 (i, ii)

How long does it take an ice cube to melt? The children could use circles divided into 12 five minute intervals to record the length of time taken for the ice cubes to melt. Order these and discuss the variation in the times. Find the range (the difference between the highest and lowest values).
National Curriculum: AT 1/2 (i, ii, iii); AT 2/2 (viii); AT 5/2 (i, ii)

Melting ice cubes Encourage the children to put their results on one sheet of paper. Was anybody's prediction exactly right? (Predicting is very difficult!) Was the ice cube in the salt water always slower or quicker to melt? Work out the difference between the quickest and slowest times for the salt water (the range). Discuss reasons for the variation.

National Curriculum: AT 1/2 (i, ii, iii); AT 2/2 (viii); AT 5/2 (i, ii, iii)

Meal sort The children may like to discuss which categories were the most difficult to fill – and why. Why do some of the meals fit in all the categories? What is the favourite breakfast, and so on? Collages of favourite meals could be made and displayed with significant meal times.
National Curriculum: AT 1/2 (i, ii, iii); AT 5/2 (iv)

Cartoon count-up The children can discuss the number of cartoon characters. They can make a block graph showing how many there are of each type. Perhaps they can sort these characters into overlapping sets according to their attributes; for example, 'runs fast', 'has big ears' or 'is a superhero'.
National Curriculum: AT 1/2 (i); AT 5/1 (i)

Likely line Encourage the children to compare their lines. Make a huge, brightly coloured class line that goes around the wall. Discuss how likely or unlikely some of the things on the display are to happen. Can the children estimate the chances of any of them (for example, an even chance)?
National Curriculum: AT 1/2 (ii); AT 5/2 (v)

Initial chance The children can discuss their findings in groups. What factors make a difference? Does it matter how many people are in the family? Talk about what happens if there are only two people. What about a family of six? This can lead into a discussion of the odds of getting your own initials – as one in two or one in six.
National Curriculum: AT 1/2 (ii); AT 5/2 (v)

Heads roll! The children can play this game again in class in pairs and record their throws. How many heads do they throw all together? How many tails? If you collect up all the class data, does it come out at about half-and-half? Talk about even chances.
National Curriculum: AT 1/2 (ii); AT 5/3 (v, vi, vii)

Butter-side down! Let the children work in groups to make large charts showing all their

trials and the outcomes. How many times did the toast fall in all? How many times was it butter-side down? Discuss the likelihood – in general terms – of it falling the right way up.
National Curriculum: AT 1/2 (i, ii); AT 5/2 (v)

Cups and coins Play a similar game in class using bricks instead of coins. Put one brick under one cup, two under another and so on. If the children guess the number of bricks correctly, they keep the bricks. Replace the missing bricks and the game can go on. The first child to collect ten bricks wins. Talk about the value of coins – which is worth most, least and so on?
National Curriculum: AT 1/1 (ii); AT 2/1 (i, ii, v); AT 5/1 (iv)

Shoe chances The children can put their results together by adding up the total number of trials, working in groups or as a class. They can then collate all the information into two columns – the number of correct shoes taken out and the number of incorrect shoes. How many are there in each column? What result do they think they should have?
National Curriculum: AT 1/2 (i, ii); AT 5/2 (v)

Bag of socks The children can discuss how likely they are to get a pair. Does it make any difference how many socks there are in the bag? If they have fewer, is it easier or harder to get a pair? What about if they have more? Try the game in class with various numbers of socks. What happens if there is an odd sock in the bag?
National Curriculum: AT 1/2 (i, ii); AT 5/3 (v, vi)

Fair's fair! The children can discuss the things they thought were unfair and those they thought were fair. Collect all their ideas up into two class books – a 'fair' book and an 'unfair' book. Think about what is necessary for the throw of a dice, the dealing of cards or the giving out of money to be fair.
National Curriculum: AT 1/2 (ii); AT 5/3 (vi)

Head talk Let the children play this game again in class. What would happen if they changed the number of coins and played with eight rather than six? Would their scores increase or go down? In their experience of playing the game, what are the likely scores? How do they judge this?
National Curriculum: AT 1/2 (i, ii); AT 5/2 (v)

Chancey square The children will need to collate all their data. Working in groups – probably based around different coins – they can work out how many rolls were successful and how many rolls were not. Were some coins 'better' at rolling than others? Talk about the chances (in rough figures) of getting the coin in the square.
National Curriculum: AT 1/2 (i, ii); AT 2/2 (iii); AT 5/3 (v, vi)

Colour luck The children can play a more complex version of this game in class with two more colours and a scoring system. In this way they will practise addition, as well as the probability aspects. Discuss why some colours (for example, blue and red) are more likely than others (for example, green and yellow).
National Curriculum: AT 1/1 (ii); AT 5/2 (v)

Hand of cards The children can play this game in class with a line of cards spread out in front of them face down. Try varying the number of each sort of card – use two 5s, for example. Do the children realise that this makes it *more* likely that a card will be a five? This game is also good for number recognition.
National Curriculum: AT 1/1 (ii); AT 2/1 (i); AT 5/1 (iv)

impact MATHS HOMEWORK

Inside out

● How quickly can you turn your clothes the right way round? You will need to be timed.

● Try three times on two separate days.

● Record your results below. Did you get faster?

Dear Parent or Carer

Children often find getting dressed after a PE lesson difficult. Please show your child how to turn articles of clothing the right way before beginning to time them. Help them to turn everything inside out first. Please help your child with the recording.

National Curriculum reference: AT 1, AT 2 and AT 5

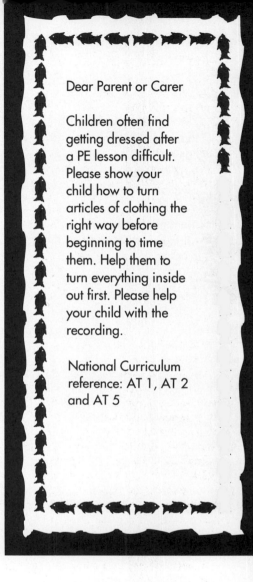

_____and

child

_____

helper(s)

_____

did this activity together

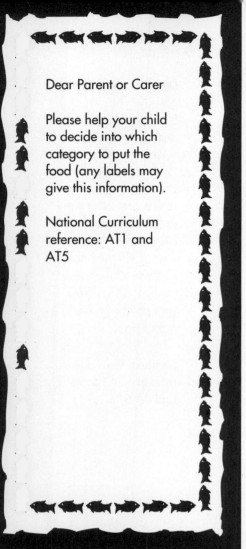

Dear Parent or Carer

Please help your child to decide into which category to put the food (any labels may give this information).

National Curriculum reference: AT1 and AT5

_____and

child

_____

helper(s)

_____

did this activity together

Lunch-box content

● Draw the contents of your lunch-box in the right set.

Sweet food

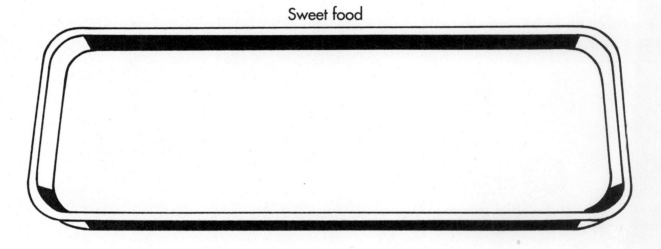

Savoury food

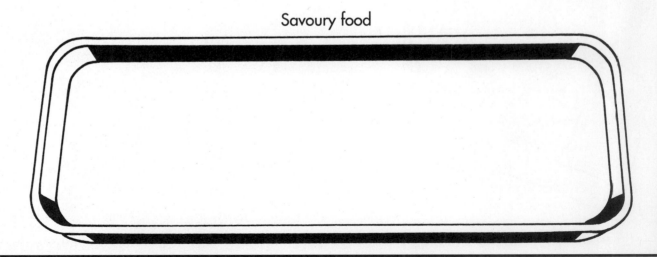

Light search

● Make a tally chart to show the number of lights in your house.

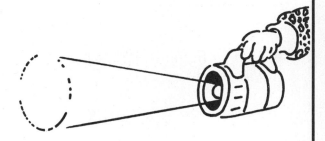

Table lamps:

Ceiling lights:

Others:

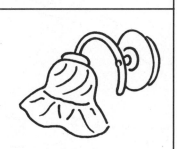

Dear Parent or Carer

Please help your child to devise a system for collecting this data.

National Curriculum reference: AT 1, AT 2 and AT 5

_____and

child

_____

helper(s)

_____

did this activity together

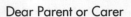

_____and

child

_____

helper(s)

_____

did this activity together

Brushes

● Find as many different brushes at home as you can.

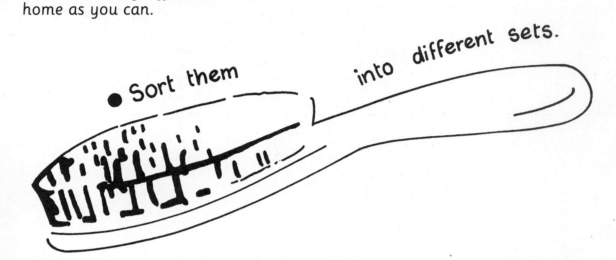

● Sort them into different sets.

● Bring to school drawings of your sets of brushes.

More than three buttons

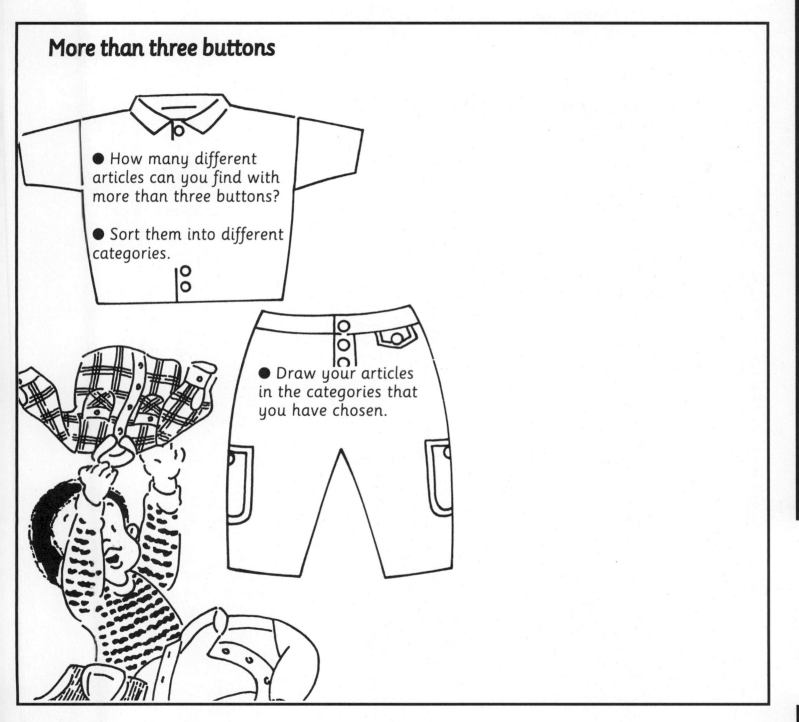

● How many different articles can you find with more than three buttons?

● Sort them into different categories.

● Draw your articles in the categories that you have chosen.

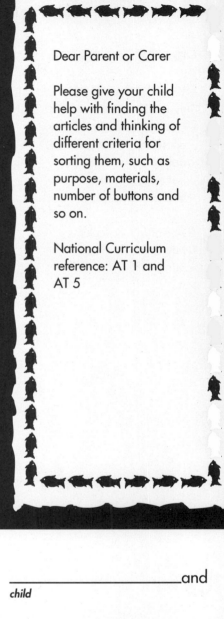

Dear Parent or Carer

Please give your child help with finding the articles and thinking of different criteria for sorting them, such as purpose, materials, number of buttons and so on.

National Curriculum reference: AT 1 and AT 5

_____and

child

_____

helper(s)

_____

did this activity together

_____and

child

_____

helper(s)

_____

did this activity together

Leaves

● Put some real leaves on to this grid.
● Try and sort your leaves so that each one is in the right space.

smooth edge

rough (not smooth) edge

shiny   **dull (not shiny)**

● Draw one leaf in each oblong and bring four leaves into school. Try and keep them flat.

impact MATHS HOMEWORK

Wheel tally

● With your helper find a safe place to make this wheel tally. You will need to time five minutes while you tally.

2 wheels:

4 wheels:

more than 4 wheels:

I began my tally at:

and finished at:

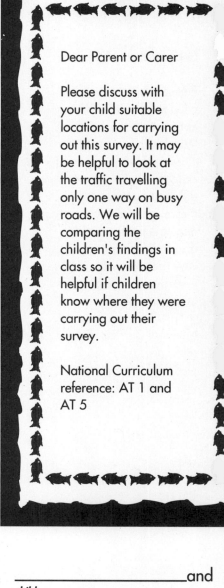

Dear Parent or Carer

Please discuss with your child suitable locations for carrying out this survey. It may be helpful to look at the traffic travelling only one way on busy roads. We will be comparing the children's findings in class so it will be helpful if children know where they were carrying out their survey.

National Curriculum reference: AT 1 and AT 5

_____and

child

_____

helper(s)

_____

did this activity together

_____and

child

_____

helper(s)

_____

did this activity together

How many tins do you open each week?

● Record the number by using a tally; for example:

cat food **|||** (3) tins each week.

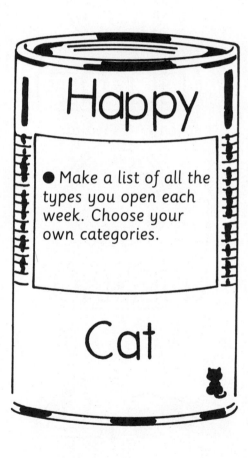

● Make a list of all the types you open each week. Choose your own categories.

Sorting money

● Please ASK if you may sort the coins in a purse or pocket.

● Make coin rubbings to show which rectangle you have put them in.

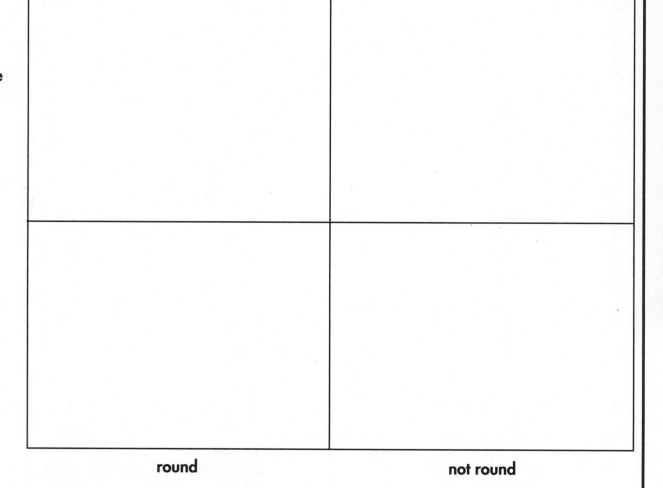

	round	not round
worth more than 15p		
worth less than 15p		

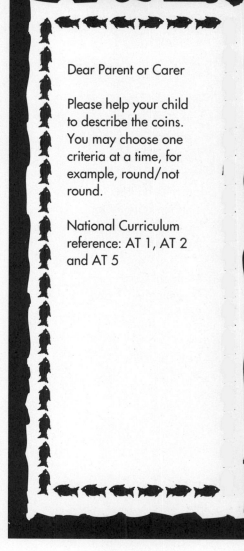

Dear Parent or Carer

Please help your child to describe the coins. You may choose one criteria at a time, for example, round/not round.

National Curriculum reference: AT 1, AT 2 and AT 5

_____and

child

_____

helper(s)

_____

did this activity together

_____and

child

_____

helper(s)

_____

did this activity together

Street survey

● Make a list of the numbers of different buildings (shops, banks and so on) in your chosen street.

Types of buildings:

● Please bring your list into school.

impact MATHS HOMEWORK

Street furniture

● Make a list of all the street furniture in your favourite street and count the numbers of each type of furniture. Use a tally chart.

• For example: bins ||| (3)

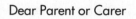

Dear Parent or Carer

Most towns have an area that has a great deal of street furniture: signposts, pedestrian crossings, flowerpots, seats and so on. Please help your child to find a suitable street to survey and to record the results.

National Curriculum reference: AT 1 and AT 5

_____and

child

_____

helper(s)

_____

did this activity together

_____and
child

_____
helper(s)

_____
did this activity together

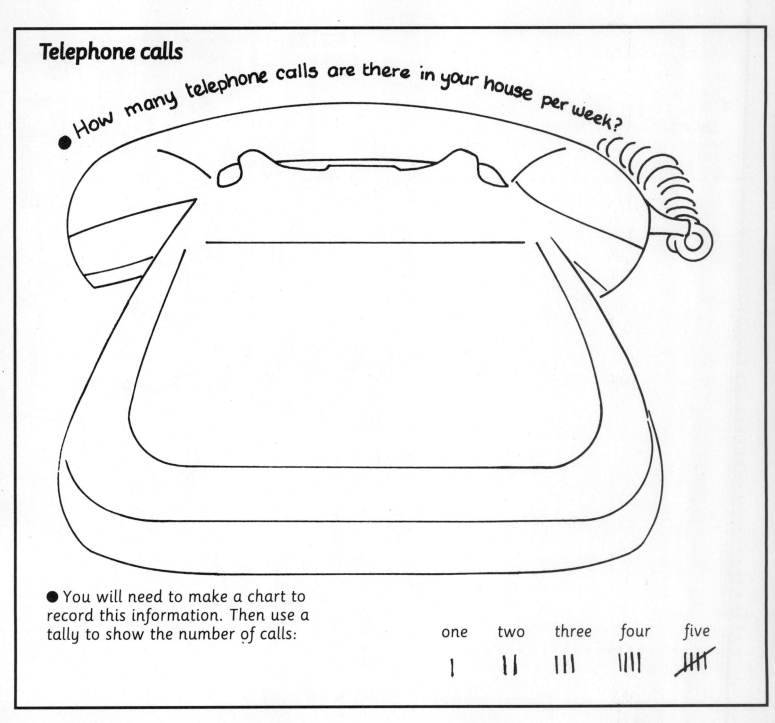

Telephone calls

● How many telephone calls are there in your house per week?

● You will need to make a chart to record this information. Then use a tally to show the number of calls:

one	two	three	four	five
I	II	III	IIII	ɫɫɫɫ

Pocket money

● Draw how much pocket money you have each week and explain how you usually spend your money?

● Please bring this information into school.

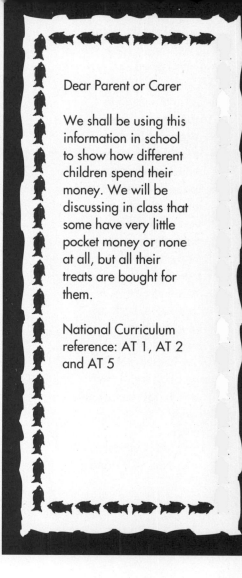

Dear Parent or Carer

We shall be using this information in school to show how different children spend their money. We will be discussing in class that some have very little pocket money or none at all, but all their treats are bought for them.

National Curriculum reference: AT 1, AT 2 and AT 5

_____and

child

_____

helper(s)

_____

did this activity together

_____and

child

_____

helper(s)

_____

did this activity together

Sorting the grocery shopping

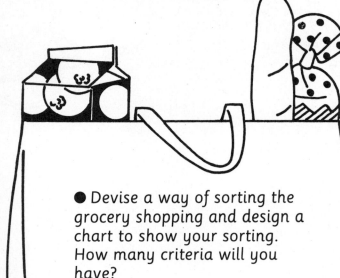

● Devise a way of sorting the grocery shopping and design a chart to show your sorting. How many criteria will you have?

● Bring your chart to school to show your method of sorting.

impact MATHS HOMEWORK

Collecting measures

● How are the amounts in the packets and containers in your home measured? Are any items measured in two ways?

● Please write the names of the items in the sets and bring any empty plastic bottles, boxes or cartons into school.

grams

millilitres

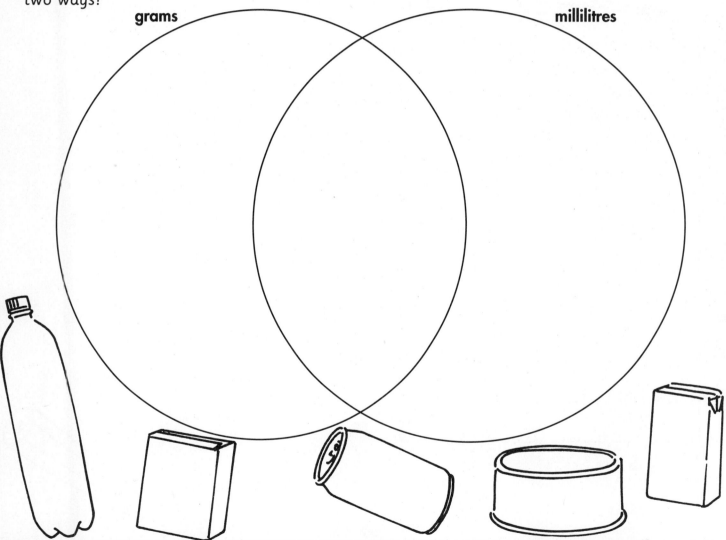

Dear Parent or Carer

Please give your child any help he or she needs to sort the containers into sets.

National Curriculum reference: AT 1, AT 2 and AT 5

_____and

child

_____

helper(s)

_____

did this activity together

Word frequency

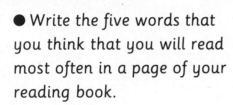

● Write the five words that you think that you will read most often in a page of your reading book.

1

2

3

4

5

● Make a tally for each of the words.

● Having read a page do you want to change any words? Try again.

1

2

3

4

5

impact MATHS HOMEWORK

Boiling a litre of water

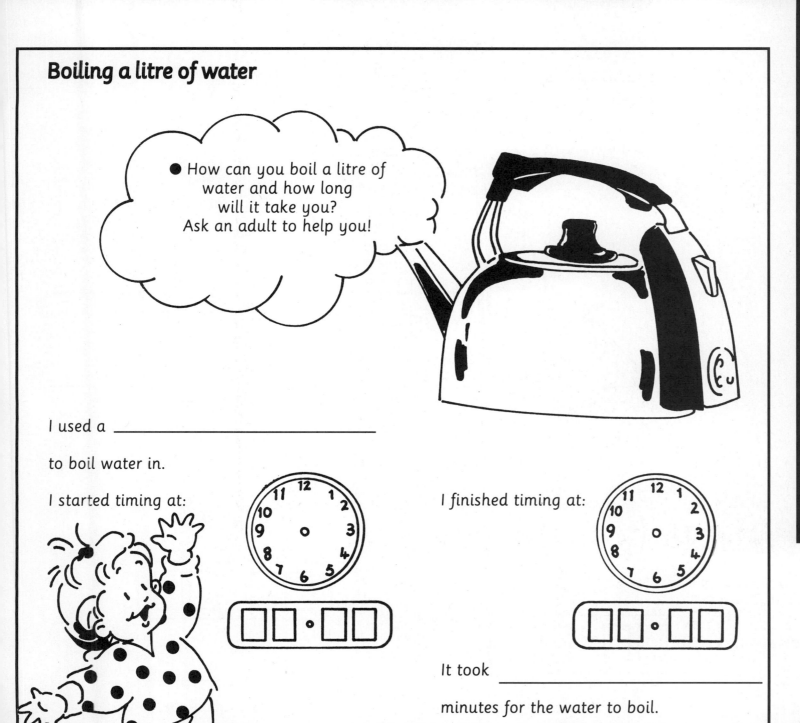

● How can you boil a litre of water and how long will it take you? Ask an adult to help you!

I used a _____

to boil water in.

I started timing at:

I finished timing at:

It took _____

minutes for the water to boil.

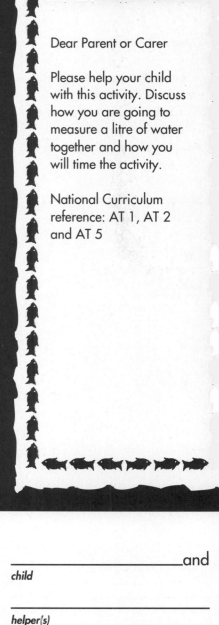

Dear Parent or Carer

Please help your child with this activity. Discuss how you are going to measure a litre of water together and how you will time the activity.

National Curriculum reference: AT 1, AT 2 and AT 5

_____ and

child

_____

helper(s)

_____

did this activity together

impact MATHS HOMEWORK

_____and

child

_____

helper(s)

_____

did this activity together

Packing your lunch-box

● Time how long it takes to prepare and pack your lunch-box.

I started at:

I finished at:

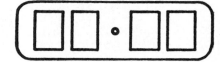

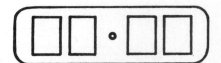

● It took _____ minutes

to prepare my lunch-box.

Car registration tally

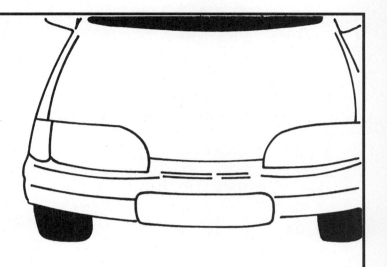

● You will need to find a safe place before beginning this activity.

● Make a tally to show in which years the cars you see were registered.

The first letter on a car or lorry registration plate will tell you the year it was registered.

A = 1983	F = 1988	L = 1993	S = 1998
B = 1984	G = 1989	M = 1994	T = 1999
C = 1985	H = 1990	N = 1995	V = 2000
D = 1986	J = 1991	P = 1996	W = 2001
E = 1987	K = 1992	R = 1997	X = 2002 ....

● Tally vehicles in a ten minute period. (For example: D cars ⦀⦀⦀⦀ 6 cars.)

Dear Parent or Carer

Your child will need help with looking at the car numbers and with the recordings. If the road is busy you will only be able to look at traffic travelling in one direction. Talk about how many cars were registered in your child's birth year. Which year is the most popular?

National Curriculum reference: AT 1, AT 2 and AT 5

_____ and

child

_____

helper(s)

_____

did this activity together

_____and

child

_____

helper(s)

_____

did this activity together

Callers

● How many people call at your house in a week? Record them on this page.

● You will need to write down each day of the week and record the calls each day. Use a tally chart:

| one || two...

● Please bring your data to school.

impact MATHS HOMEWORK

Less than £1, more than £1

● While shopping in the supermarket, write down five items in each list:

	Less than £1	
	Name of item	Price
1		
2		
3		
4		
5		

	More than £1, but less than £2	
	Name of item	Price
1		
2		
3		
4		
5		

● Please bring your information to school to share.

Dear Parent or Carer

Children often find recording money difficult, so please give your child help, if needed. Do give your child time at the supermarket to gather the information. If this is difficult, the till receipt could prove useful. Your child could use two colours, one to underline prices less than £1 and a different colour to underline prices greater than £1 but less than £2. This information will be used in school.

National Curriculum reference: AT 1, AT 2 and AT 5

_____and

child

_____

helper(s)

_____

did this activity together

Dear Parent or Carer

Please help your child with this tally. Children often need help with totalling money, so encourage your child to arrange the coins from largest to smallest in value and to make an estimate before beginning to count.

National Curriculum reference: AT 1, AT 2 and AT 5

_____and

child

_____

helper(s)

_____

did this activity together

Small change survey

● ASK if you may sort and count the coins in either a pocket or a purse every day for a week.

Day	£1	50p	20p	10p	5p	2p	1p	Total
Monday								
Tuesday								
Wednesday								
Thursday								
Friday								
Saturday								
Sunday								

impact MATHS HOMEWORK

How long does it take an ice cube to melt?

I put an ice cube on a _____ at:

I think that it will take [ ] minutes to melt.

My ice cube had melted by:

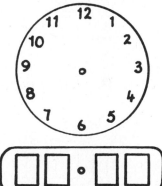

It took _____ minutes to melt.

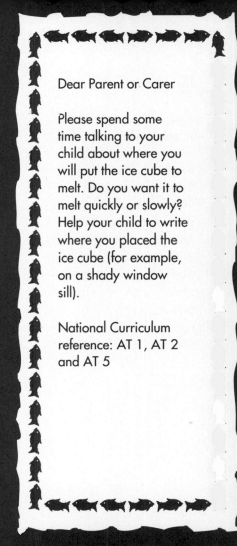

Dear Parent or Carer

Please spend some time talking to your child about where you will put the ice cube to melt. Do you want it to melt quickly or slowly? Help your child to write where you placed the ice cube (for example, on a shady window sill).

National Curriculum reference: AT 1, AT 2 and AT 5

_____ and

child

_____

helper(s)

_____

did this activity together

Dear Parent or Carer

Please help your child to set up the experiment and help them with the writing of their predictions. Talk to your child about how to make the tests fair.

National Curriculum reference: AT 1, AT 2 and AT 5

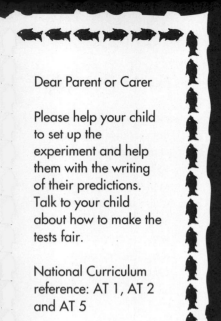

_____and

child

_____

helper(s)

_____

did this activity together

Melting ice cubes

YOU WILL NEED: two ice cubes, some salt and two jam jars half full of cold water.

● In the other jar, drop an ice cube and teaspoonful of salt.

● Drop an ice cube in one jar.

salt   Time started   no salt

I predict that it will take _____ minutes for the ice to melt.

● When did the ice cubes melt? Draw the times on the clocks.

salty water   non-salty water

impact MATHS HOMEWORK

Meal sort

● Ask your family about the meals that they enjoy eating.

● Write the meals in the set(s) in which you think that they belong.
For example: where would you write 'bacon and eggs'?

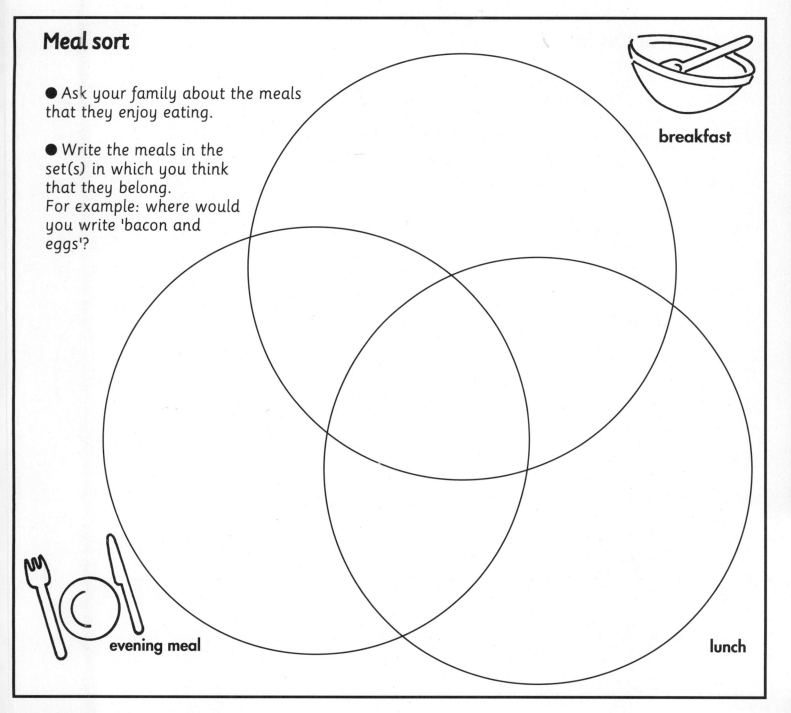

breakfast

evening meal

lunch

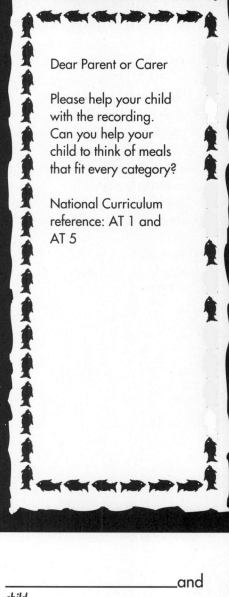

Dear Parent or Carer

Please help your child with the recording. Can you help your child to think of meals that fit every category?

National Curriculum reference: AT 1 and AT 5

_____and

child

_____

helper(s)

_____

did this activity together

_____and

child

_____

helper(s)

_____

did this activity together

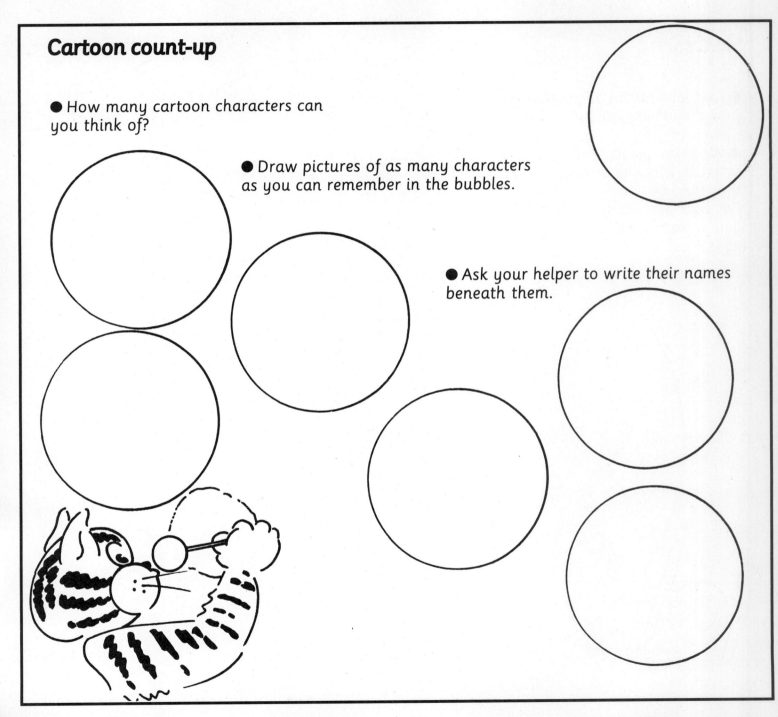

Cartoon count-up

● How many cartoon characters can you think of?

● Draw pictures of as many characters as you can remember in the bubbles.

● Ask your helper to write their names beneath them.

Likely line

● With your helper choose and draw along the line below pictures of events or things which you think are: impossible; very, very unlikely to happen and so on.

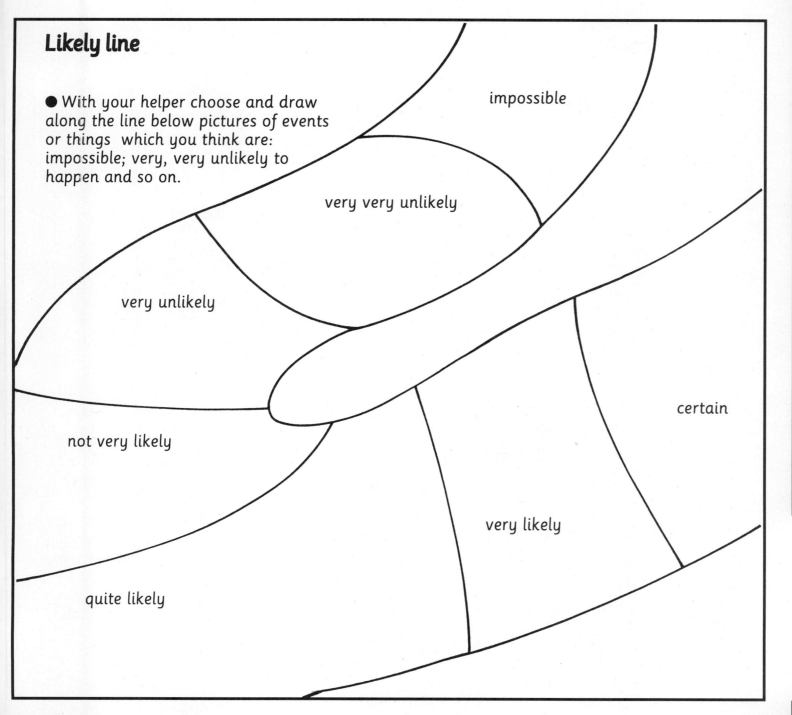

impossible

very very unlikely

very unlikely

not very likely

quite likely

certain

very likely

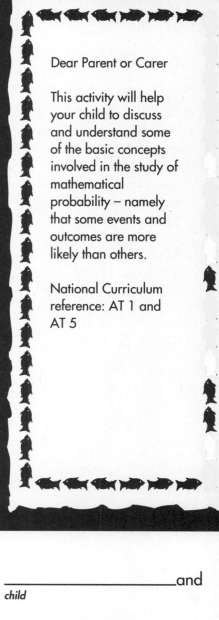

Dear Parent or Carer

This activity will help your child to discuss and understand some of the basic concepts involved in the study of mathematical probability – namely that some events and outcomes are more likely than others.

National Curriculum reference: AT 1 and AT 5

_____and

child

_____

helper(s)

_____

did this activity together

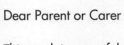
Initial chance

YOU WILL NEED: as many pieces of card as there are people in your family, crayons and a paper or coloured plastic bag.

● Write the initials of the people in your family on separate pieces of card. On each card, also draw a picture of the person.

● Put the cards in the bag and shake them up.

● Ask your family to take it in turns to take one piece out of the bag, while they have their eyes shut.

● Does anyone get their own initials?

● Try this several times and record what happens. What is the best you get (such as, two people are right and two people are wrong)? What is the worst?

● Bring your results back into school.

Heads roll!

YOU WILL NEED: a counter each and a coin.

● Choose to be either 'heads' or 'tails'. One person must be 'heads' and the other 'tails'.

● Take it in turns to spin a coin. If you are 'heads' and you spin a head, move along the track to the next 'head'. If you are 'tails' and spin a tail, move along the track to the next tail.

● If you throw three of the wrong sort in a row (that is, 'heads' when you are 'tails'), you get an extra turn.

● The first person to reach the last space is the winner.

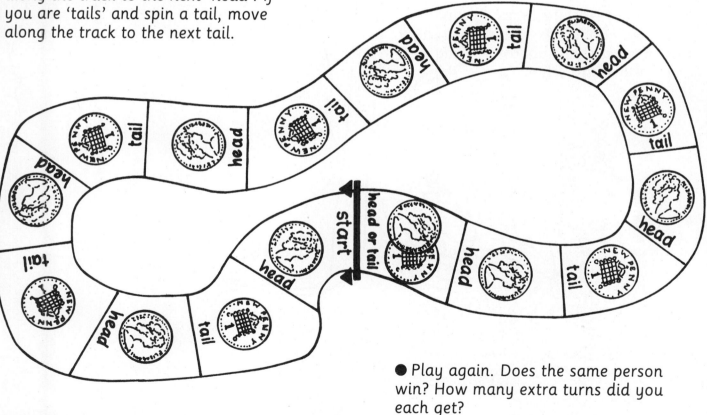

● Play again. Does the same person win? How many extra turns did you each get?

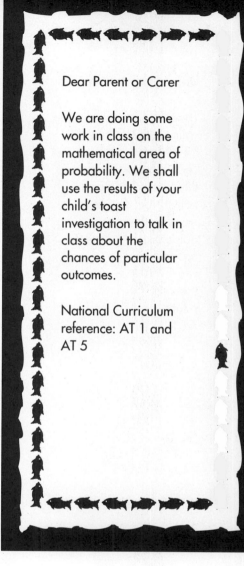

Dear Parent or Carer

We are doing some work in class on the mathematical area of probability. We shall use the results of your child's toast investigation to talk in class about the chances of particular outcomes.

National Curriculum reference: AT 1 and AT 5

_____ and

child

_____

helper(s)

_____

did this activity together

_____and

child

_____

helper(s)

_____

did this activity together

Butter-side down!

If you drop a piece of toast, how likely is it to fall butter-side down?

● Try this out. Ask an adult to help you make a piece of buttered toast. Don't make it too buttery!

● Drop it on to a plate or tray, so that it doesn't make a mess.

● Drop it at least 12 times. Record which way up it falls each time in the slice of toast shape opposite. Bring your results into school.

impact MATHS HOMEWORK

Cups and coins

YOU WILL NEED: some cups and as many different sorts of coins as you can find.

● Study the coins carefully. Make sure that you know what they are called.

● Ask someone to put a different coin under each cup without you watching!

● Point at a cup and guess what coin is underneath it. Lift up that cup and look.

● If you are right, take the coin. If you are wrong, put the cup back and try another cup.

● Keep guessing until you have collected all the coins.

● How many guesses did it take for you to collect all the coins? Play again. Can you do better this time?

Dear Parent or Carer

This activity will help your child with coin recognition, but it will also help him or her to develop the basic idea of probability or likelihood. Which coin is *likely* to be under this cup? Encourage your child to think about his or her guesses.

National Curriculum reference: AT 1, AT 2 and AT 5

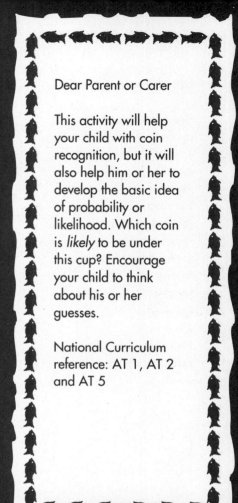

_____and

child

_____

helper(s)

_____

did this activity together

impact MATHS HOMEWORK

_____and

child

_____

helper(s)

_____

did this activity together

Shoe chances

If I am feeling for my slippers in the dark, how likely is it that I will put my foot into the correct shoe for that foot? That is, how likely am I to put my left foot into the left slipper?

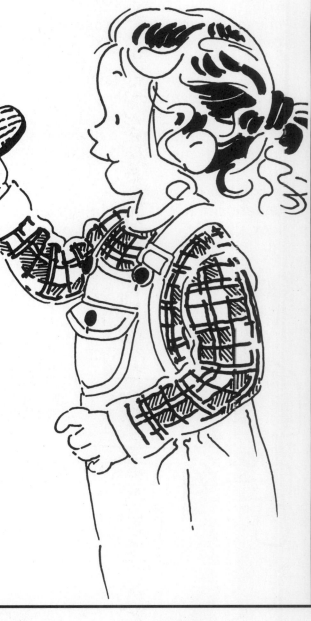

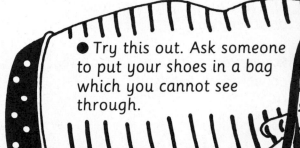

● Try this out. Ask someone to put your shoes in a bag which you cannot see through.

● Shutting your eyes, say which shoe you want (that is, the right or the left) and then take one out.
● Open your eyes. Is it the one you wanted?
● Try this at least six times and record what happens opposite. Bring your results into school.

impact MATHS HOMEWORK

Bag of socks

- Find as many pairs of socks as you can and put them in a plastic or paper bag which you cannot see through.

- Without looking, take it in turns to pick out two socks. If they are a pair, you may keep them. If not, put them back.

- Keep playing until all the socks have been picked out.

- Who has the most pairs?

(If possible, wear gloves for this activity – it prevents cheating!)

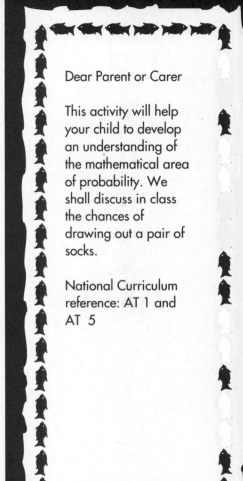

Dear Parent or Carer

This activity will help your child to develop an understanding of the mathematical area of probability. We shall discuss in class the chances of drawing out a pair of socks.

National Curriculum reference: AT 1 and AT 5

_____and

child

_____

helper(s)

_____

did this activity together

_____and

child

_____

helper(s)

_____

did this activity together

Fair's fair!

● Think of at least three things or events that you think were or are unfair. Draw them in the appropriate space below.

● Think of three things or events which you think are fair. Draw these in the appropriate space below.

These are UNFAIR

These are FAIR

impact MATHS HOMEWORK

Head talk

YOU WILL NEED: six coins.

● Count the coins. Throw them up in the air. How many land 'heads'? Move those coins to one side.

● Throw the rest in the air. Move those which land 'heads' to one side again. If there are any left, throw them in the air again.

● Any which finally land 'tails' you can count as your score.

● So, if one coin is 'tails', score 1. If two are 'tails', score 2, and so on. Then let your partner have a turn. Play until one of you has scored 5 points. That person wins.

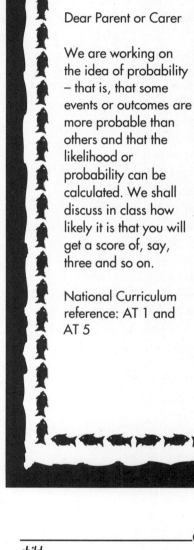

Dear Parent or Carer

We are working on the idea of probability – that is, that some events or outcomes are more probable than others and that the likelihood or probability can be calculated. We shall discuss in class how likely it is that you will get a score of, say, three and so on.

National Curriculum reference: AT 1 and AT 5

_____and

child

_____

helper(s)

_____

did this activity together

_____and

child

_____

helper(s)

_____

did this activity together

Chancey square

YOU WILL NEED: a coin.

● Put the other piece of paper in the middle of a table. Take it in turns to roll the coin along the table and on to the paper. Does it land in the square?

● Have ten turns at rolling the coin. Each time it lands in the square give yourself a score of the value of the coin. (For example, if you are rolling a 10p piece, score 10p each time it lands in the square.)

● Write down your score.

● How much could you have scored, if your coin had landed in the square all ten times?

● Bring both figures into school.

impact MATHS HOMEWORK

Chancey square

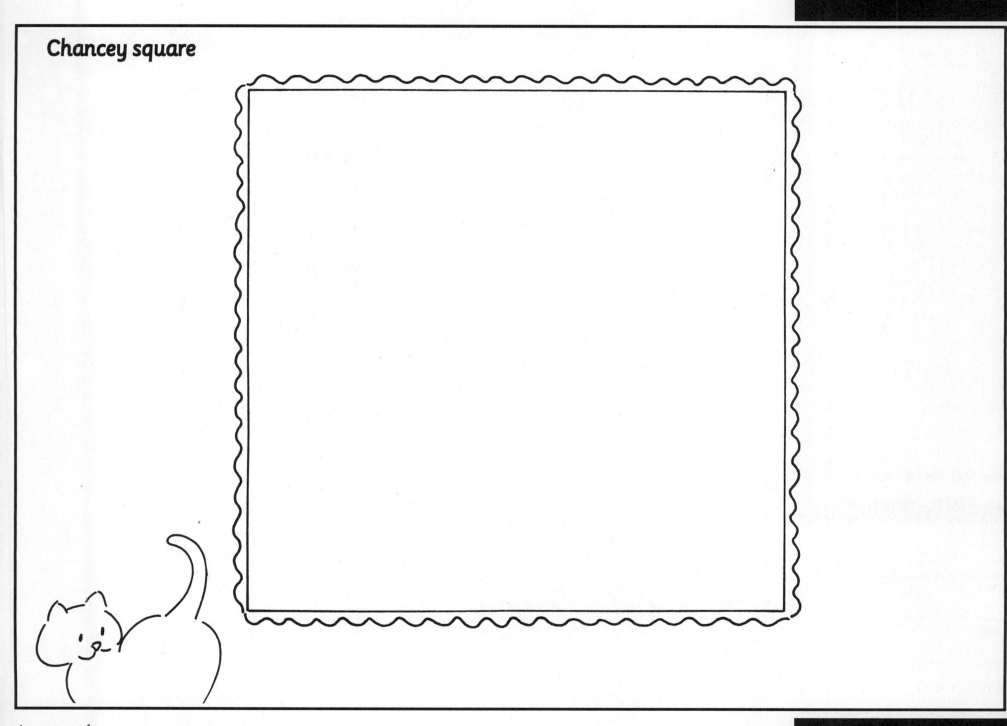

_____and

child

_____

helper(s)

_____

did this activity together

Colour luck

YOU WILL NEED: some small coloured pieces of card – two blue, two red, one yellow and one green – coloured on one side only. (They could be made out of the back of an old birthday or Christmas card.)

● Place the cards in a pile face down.

● Take it in turns to turn over one card. Before you turn it over, say what colour you think it will be. If you are right, keep it!

● Does it get easier to guess?

● By the end who has the most cards?

● Play several times. Try scoring as follows: 2 points for blue or red and 1 point for green or yellow. The winner is the one who has the highest score.

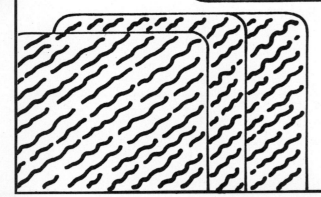

impact MATHS HOMEWORK

Hand of cards

YOU WILL NEED: five playing cards (with numbers on) and a pile of counters (for example small bricks).

● Hold the cards in your hand, so that your helper cannot see them.

● Tell your helper what numbers are on the cards.

● Your helper should point to one of the cards and say what number they think it is. If they are right, they can take a counter and you should put the card face up on the table. If they are wrong, you take a counter.

● Your helper should then point to another card and say what number they think it is. If they are right, they take a counter and you put the card face up on the table. If they are wrong, you take a counter.

● They should keep pointing and guessing until they have discovered which card is which.

● How many counters have you each got when all five cards are face up?

● Now let your helper hold the five cards and you do the guessing. Who wins this time?

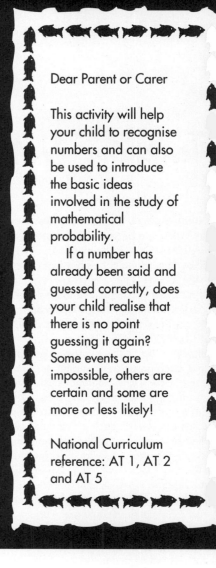

Dear Parent or Carer

This activity will help your child to recognise numbers and can also be used to introduce the basic ideas involved in the study of mathematical probability.
    If a number has already been said and guessed correctly, does your child realise that there is no point guessing it again? Some events are impossible, others are certain and some are more or less likely!

National Curriculum reference: AT 1, AT 2 and AT 5

_____and

child

_____

helper(s)

_____

did this activity together

Teachers' Notes
YEAR TWO

Number plates The number plates they have recorded can be sorted into those that use the same number combinations. Are there some number combinations that have not been found? Is there any way of finding out what these missing combinations are? Display all the different combinations.
National Curriculum: AT 1/2 (i, ii, iii); AT 2/2 (i, iii); AT 5/2 (i)

Sharing 10p Sit the children in groups of five, each group using a different coin value. How many different ways are there of sharing the total using just 1p coins? Are there more combinations if a mixture of coins is allowed? Each group could record their favourite way of sharing the coins. Try larger coin values or vary the group numbers.
National Curriculum: AT 1/2 (i, ii, iii); AT 2/2 (iii, v); AT 5/2 (i)

How many different sorts of beans can you find? The children could make up the prices with money, and the tins could be used for shopping activities. How many different sorts of baked beans did they find? Are other types of beans packed in tins?
National Curriculum: AT 1/2 (i, ii, iii); 2/2 (iii, v); 5/2 (i)

Dairy products Discuss the differences between solids and liquids and how their states can be changed. Investigate the changes when water is heated and cooled. Ask questions such as 'What happens to the water in the clothes on the washing line?'
National Curriculum: AT 1/2 (i, ii, iii); AT 5/2 (i)

Going shopping The children can gather the information for individual days, whole weeks and so on. This can be displayed in a variety of ways suggested by the children. The shopping can be categorised into essential and non-essential and displayed as a Venn diagram.
National Curriculum: AT 1/2 (i, ii, iii); AT 2/2 (iii, viii); AT 5/2 (i, ii, iii)

Reading time The children may like to make a list of all the activities that their family do which involve reading. Are these activities necessary or for pleasure? Choose six stories that are enjoyed by the children. Make a tally to find out their order of preference for the stories.
National Curriculum: AT 1/2 (i, ii, iii); AT 2/2 (iii, viii); AT 5/2 (i, ii, iii)

Words The children could order their words in different ways (say alphabetical order or by the number of letters in words) and list them. Groups could work on separate totals: total score for four-letter words, total for words beginning with different letters and so on. Their lists could be displayed using different criteria.
National Curriculum: AT 1/2 (i, ii, iii); AT 2/2 (i, iii); AT 5/2 (ii)

Lunch-box cost Ask the children to find the total cost of the contents of their lunch-boxes. Can they make their total amounts using the least number of coins? Who used the least coins? Working in pairs, let them find the differences between the total costs of their lunches. How much change would they get from £1? Display all their information and work in a class book.
National Curriculum: AT 1/2 (i, ii, iii); AT 2/2 (iii, v); AT 5/2 (ii)

Monday's child is...? Once this information has been entered on to a computer database, encourage the children to interpret the data by asking questions such as 'On which day were most children born? Were more children born at night or during the day? How many children were born at the weekend?' This information can be displayed alongside the poem, 'Monday's child'.
National Curriculum: AT 1/2 (ii); AT 2/2 (viii); 5/3 (i, ii)

My school coat The children can work in small groups to collect and display the information. Let each group choose a way to display their information. Which displays are the easiest to interpret? Why?
National Curriculum: AT 1/3 (i, ii, iv); AT 5/3 (i, ii, iii)

My front door The children could enter all their information on to a database program to interpret it. Discuss why are some materials more popular than others? Do the materials used restrict colour choices? Which position is best for a letter box?
National Curriculum: AT 1/3 (i, ii); AT 4/1 (ii); AT 5/3 (i, ii, iii)

School time, sleep time The children could order the information to find out how long they spend in bed. A large 24 hour clock could be made and significant times could be put on to it. The 'School time, sleep time' clocks from individual children's sheets could be placed near with questions, for example, 'How many more hours do we spend sleeping than at school in a week? How many hours do we sleep in a week?'
National Curriculum: AT 1/3 (iii); AT 2/3 (x); AT 5/3 (i, iv)

Getting ready for school The children should be asked what problems they encountered during the investigation and how they overcame them. They could enter their information on to a computer database and print it out in graph form.
National Curriculum: AT 1/3 (i, ii, iii); AT 5/3 (ii, iii)

Switch it on! This information could be entered, displayed and investigated on a computer database. Which electrical items are seen to be essential? Why? Are there alternative sources of power for some items?
National Curriculum: AT 1/2 (i, ii); AT 5/3 (ii, iii)

Shoelace tying competition The children could find the differences between their fastest and slowest times. These could be ordered to show the greatest improvement. Can everyone tie laces or be able to learn in the next two weeks?
National Curriculum: AT 1/3 (i, ii, iv); AT 2/3 (x, xi); AT 5/3 (i, ii)

Making an ice cube The children could make time lines demarcated into five minute intervals (for example, one LEGO brick represents five minutes) to record the time taken for their liquids to freeze. These could be displayed in order and the differences discussed and explained. How many ice cubes took more than an hour to freeze? Did it depend on the size of the ice cube? This could lead to further investigation.
National Curriculum: AT 1/3 (ii, iii, iv); AT 2/3 (x); AT 5/3 (ii, iii, iv)

Take a seat The children could use the computer to enter their data and answer questions on it. They could investigate why certain heights are used for chairs of a particular purpose. Are all the school chairs the same height? Why not? Are the school chairs coded? What is the order of the code? Do the chairs reflect the heights of the tables?
National Curriculum: AT 1/2 (i, ii); AT 5/3 (ii, iii)

How much milk do you drink in a week? The various types and amount of milk consumed could be entered into a database. Then the information could be printed out. Why does the milkman charge more for his milk than the supermarket? What are the advantages and/or disadvantages of doorstep delivery?
National Curriculum: AT 1/2 (i, ii); AT 2/2 (ii); AT 5/3 (i, ii, iii)

School, TV, sleep Discuss how many of the children spend more time at school than watching TV, and whether this is different for older/younger children girls/boys. Display the results in a class book, near a large 24 hour clock illustrating school and night-time activities.
National Curriculum: AT 1/3 (ii); AT 2/3 (x); AT 5/3 (i, iv)

Screw-top survey In PE, the children could illustrate with their bodies the number of turns taken to remove the tops. The whole class could repeat the turns before trying a different top. Young children could talk about ¾ turns or 2 whole turns. Older children could learn about degrees. Can the children predict how many turns will be needed by examining the threads?
National Curriculum: AT 1/3 (i, ii); AT 5/3 (i)

How far to work? This information could be used in a variety of ways once it has been entered on to the computer. Consider questions such as, 'How many people travel to work by train and take more than 30 minutes? Which mode of transport is the quickest? Do some people travel by more than one method? Why?'
National Curriculum: AT 1/3 (i, ii); AT 2/3 (xi); AT 5/3 (i, ii, iii)

Holidays Let the children find their holiday destinations on a map. Discuss distances and modes of transport. Display the class's holiday destinations for that year on a large map. The means of travel could be categorised and displayed as a border around it.
National Curriculum: AT 1/3 (i, ii); AT 2/3 (xi); AT 5/3 (iv)

Cornflakes The children could work in groups, using a calculator, in order to establish which size and brand is the best value. This information could be entered on to a computer database and information extracted. This activity could be extended to other supermarket produce such as crisps or chocolate bars.
National Curriculum: AT 1/3 (i, ii, iii, iv); AT 2/3 (xi); AT 5/3 (ii, iii, iv)

Milk prices The children can work in groups to collate and present the information as charts which can be interpreted. The cartons can be used in a 'dairy shop' or as part of a data display.
National Curriculum: AT 1/3 (i, ii); AT 2/2 (vii); AT 5/3 (i, ii)

Five minutes peace The children can perform a variety of five-minute tasks in class; for example, how many sums can they do or how many different words can they write in five minutes? They can categorise all their information about what they did in their five minutes silence under various headings, such as reading or watching TV. This information can then be represented either on a block graph (if there are more than three categories) or on a Venn diagram.
National Curriculum: AT 1/2 (ii); AT 2/2 (viii); AT 5/2 (i, ii)

Colour chance Working in groups, the children can make a giant 'spinner' for display purposes. They can count up between them the number of times that their spinners landed on red, green, blue and yellow and write their totals on to the giant spinner. Count up the total number of spins. The overall probability *should* then come out at about one quarter on each colour. If it does not, what do the children think might be the causes? Talk about 'fair' spinners.
National Curriculum: AT 1/2 (i, ii); AT 5/3 (v, vi, vii)

Lucky aces The children can collate all their information, first working in groups and then putting together the groups' results. How many times were the cards thrown in all? How many landed face up in all? What are the chances of a card landing face up? Look at those that did land face up. What are the chances of the face up card being the ace of spades or the ace of hearts? Discuss this.
National Curriculum: AT 1/2 (i, ii); AT 5/3 (v, vi)

Open book When the children bring their figures back into school, talk about them as a class. Are there any patterns? Do some books open more than once – even several times – at the same page? Discuss why this might be. With a ten-page book, what are the chances of opening it any any one page? Is there any such thing as a random opening?
National Curriculum: AT 1/2 (i, ii); AT 5/3 (v, vi)

Chatterbox The children can make a chart showing the numbers of minutes and seconds people managed to talk without saying the words 'yes' or 'no'. How many people tried it in all? How many of them succeeded? Roughly speaking, what are the chances of success? Discuss the accuracy of the timing and other factors which might affect whether you can succeed or not.
National Curriculum: AT 1/3 (i, ii); AT 2/3 (xi); AT 5/3 (v, vi)

Page view The children may need to choose a book from school to take home so that they can do this activity. When they bring their findings into school, discuss how likely or unlikely each outcome was. Working in groups, the children can categorise each of their 'random openings' as likely, unlikely or very unlikely. Can they give an idea of how probable it was in their particular book that they would open it on a page with a 'the'?
National Curriculum: AT 1/3 (i, ii); AT 5/3 (v, vi)

Head start The children can work together in groups to produce a chart collating their results. Draw a graph showing how many throws were needed to get four heads in a row. What was the most and the least? Can the children work out how many throws *should* be needed, mathematically speaking?
National Curriculum: AT 1/2 (i, ii, iii); AT 5/2 (v)

Letter chances Try playing this game in class and use the letters to make words. Clearly you will have to choose the letters to go in the bag carefully. What if there is more than one of a particular letter? Does this make it more likely that they will withdraw that one? Give the letters scores, as in 'Scrabble', how much can the children score?
National Curriculum: AT 1/2 (ii); AT 5/2 (v)

Red winner Encourage the children to play the game again in class. What happens if more colours are introduced? What if the game is made very simple and they only have two colours? Talk about why more of the same colour would make a difference.

The children could record their scores and see who gets the highest.
National Curriculum: AT 1/2 (ii); AT 5/2 (v)

Number chances The children can play the game in class, recording the cards they take and how many turns they need to have to choose all the odd numbers. When everyone has played it at least once, look at the results. How many turns does it usually take to finish the game? How good are your chances of finishing the game in ten turns, or in eight turns?
National Curriculum: AT 1/2 (ii); AT 3/2 (ii); AT 5/2 (v)

Coin sandwich The children can throw coins in class and record their outcomes. Can they see which outcomes are easier to get and why? Let them experiment with scoring, for example giving heads and tails different values (5 for a head, 4 for a tail and so on). Ask them to score each turn and add their scores. Who reaches 50 first?
National Curriculum: AT 1/2 (i, ii); AT 5/2 (v)

Card shuffle The children can play the same game in class against themselves, recording the numbers of turns they have in order to collect all the cards. How good can they get at this game? Is it all luck? They can play against each other and add up the numbers on their cards as scores. What about adding some larger numbers to the pack?
National Curriculum: AT 1/2 (ii); AT 2/1 (i); AT 5/2 (v)

Spinning maths The children can use their spinners in class and try out each others. Do they recognise that the spinner is more likely to land on the colour of the largest area? Ask them to make some spinners with eight segments, colouring three segments in one colour and the rest in different colours. What does this do to the chances of getting a particular colour? Talk about this.
National Curriculum: AT 1/1 (i, ii); AT 2/2 (vi); AT 5/2 (v)

_____and

child

_____

helper(s)

_____

did this activity together

Number plates

● Can you find a number plate on a car
where the numbers add up to 14?
For example: F365 VWL
3 + 6 + 5 = 14

I started this activity at:

● Try to find two number plates which
do this.

I finished finding the number plates at:

impact MATHS HOMEWORK

Sharing 10p

● How many different ways can you share 10p between five people?

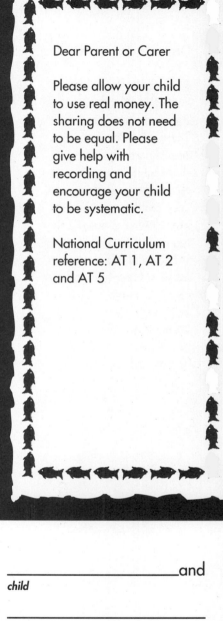

Dear Parent or Carer

Please allow your child to use real money. The sharing does not need to be equal. Please give help with recording and encourage your child to be systematic.

National Curriculum reference: AT 1, AT 2 and AT 5

_____ and

child

_____

helper(s)

_____

did this activity together

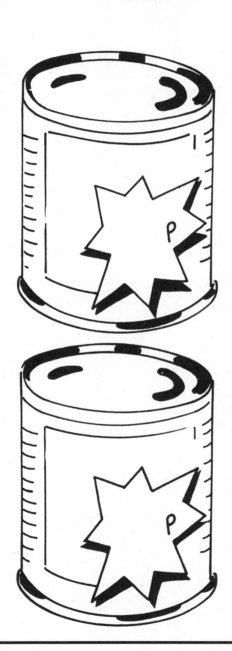
_____and

child

_____

helper(s)

_____

did this activity together

How many different sorts of beans can you find?

● Write out the different sorts of beans and the price on each of the tins.

● Cut out your tins and place them in price order.

Dairy products

● Draw or write as many dairy products as possible on to this diagram.

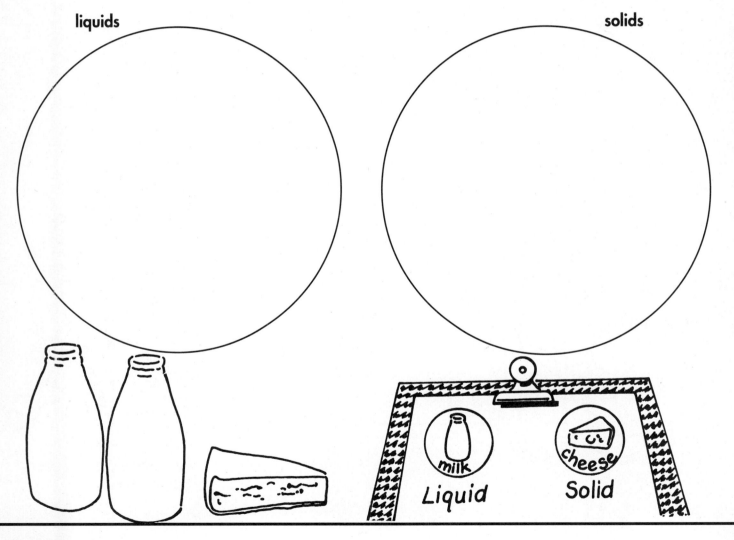

liquids

solids

Dear Parent or Carer

You will need to discuss the differences between a solid and a liquid before you begin the task. Please give your child time to look at the dairy products at home or the shops. Help may be needed with recording the information needed.

National Curriculum reference: AT 1 and AT 5

_____and

child

_____

helper(s)

_____

did this activity together

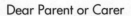
Going shopping

● How many hours does your family spend shopping every week?

impact MATHS HOMEWORK

Reading time

● How long do you spend reading? What about the other members of your family?

● Ask your family to record all the time that they spend reading in one day.

● Bring your information to school.

_____and

child

_____

helper(s)

_____

did this activity together

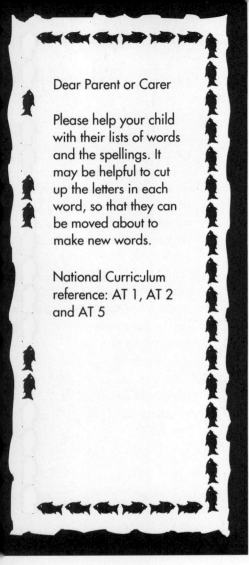

_____and

child

_____

helper(s)

_____

did this activity together

Words

● How many smaller words can you make using the letters in these two big words? Use each word separately and make two lists.

England

because

● Which word gets the highest total score?

● Bring your lists into school.

● Score 2 points for two-letter words, 3 points for three-letter words and so on.

impact MATHS HOMEWORK

Lunch-box cost

- Draw pictures of everything in your lunch-box.

- Alongside each item, draw the amount of money needed to purchase it.

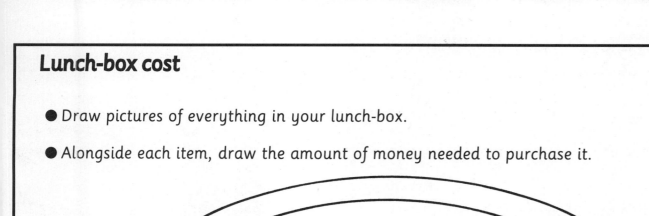

Dear Parent or Carer

Please allow your child to place real money alongside each item of food. Encourage them to discuss the different values of the coins and the price of the food. They could arrange the items in price order before beginning their recording.

National Curriculum reference: AT 1, AT 2 and AT 5

_____and

child

_____

helper(s)

_____

did this activity together

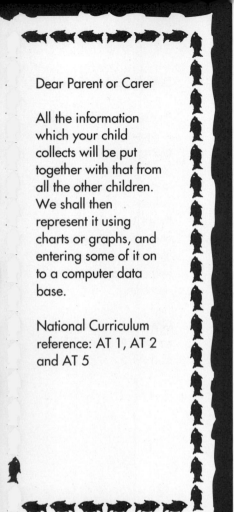
_____and

child

_____

helper(s)

_____

did this activity together

Monday's child is...?

● On which day of the week were you born?

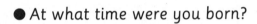

● At what time were you born?

● Where were you born?

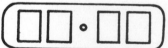

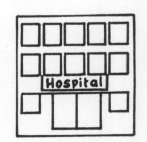

My school coat

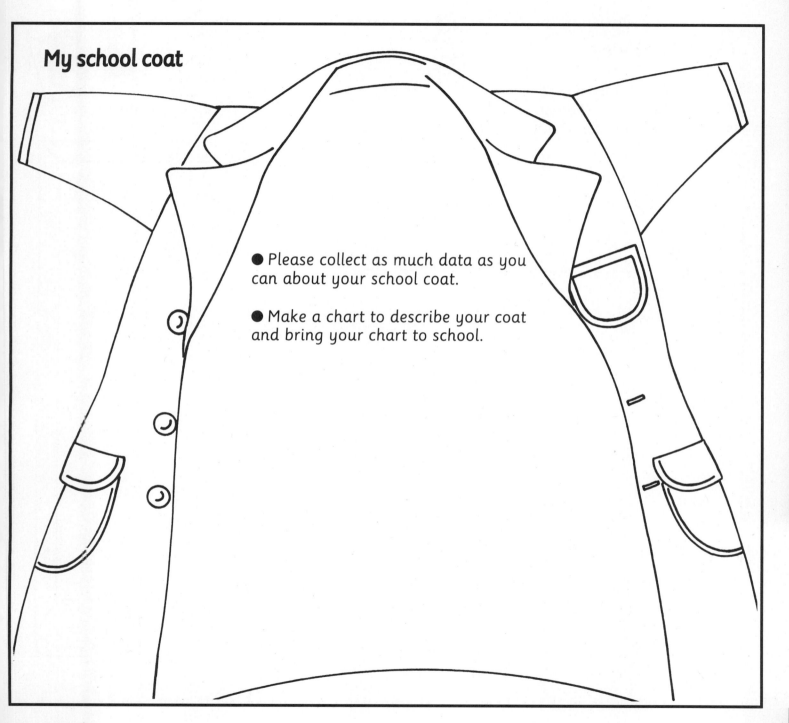

- Please collect as much data as you can about your school coat.

- Make a chart to describe your coat and bring your chart to school.

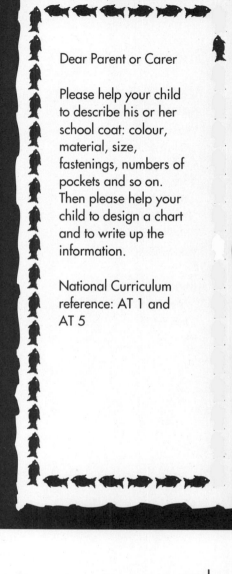

Dear Parent or Carer

Please help your child to describe his or her school coat: colour, material, size, fastenings, numbers of pockets and so on. Then please help your child to design a chart and to write up the information.

National Curriculum reference: AT 1 and AT 5

_____and

child

_____

helper(s)

_____

did this activity together

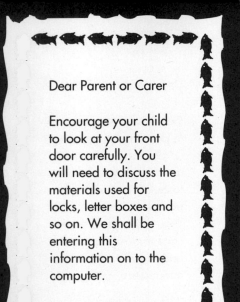

_____and

child

_____

helper(s)

_____

did this activity together

My front door

LETTERS

● Design a chart in the space below to show everything about your front door: materials, number, letter box, locks and so on.

● Draw your front door in this frame.

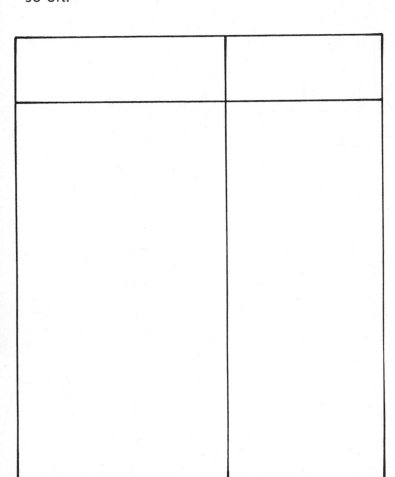

WELCOME

impact MATHS HOMEWORK

School time, sleep time

24 hour clock

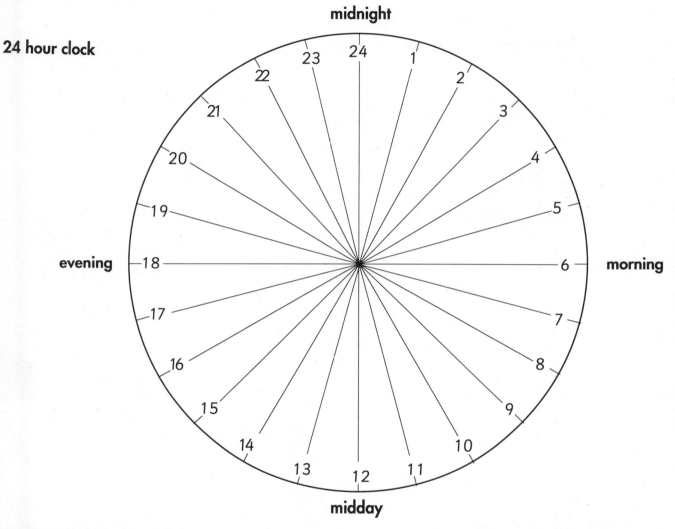

YOU WILL NEED: two different coloured crayons or felt-tipped pens.

● Use one colour to shade in the number of hours that you sleep and use the other colour to shade in the number of hours that you are at school each day.

● Bring your information to school.

Dear Parent or Carer

You will need to discuss the 24 hour clock with your child. He or she will need to know that the hour hand on a normal, 12 hour clock goes round twice in a day, but only once on a 24 hour clock. Your child might like to consider how long other members of the family spend sleeping or at work.

National Curriculum reference: AT 1, AT 2 and AT 5

_____and

child

_____

helper(s)

_____

did this activity together

_____and

child

_____

helper(s)

_____

did this activity together

Getting ready for school

● How long does it take to get ready for school/work?

● Time everyone at home getting ready for school or work and bring your timings into school.

Name	Time they took to get ready (in minutes)
me	

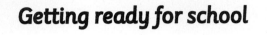

impact MATHS HOMEWORK

Switch it on!

- How many things at home use electricity?

- Make a list of everything at home that uses electricity and bring the list to school.

Dear Parent or Carer

You may like to help your child to group the equipment into different categories such as: things which are used to heat something up or cool something down, things which do some 'work' and things which provide 'light'.

National Curriculum reference: AT 1 and AT 5

_____and

child

_____

helper(s)

_____

did this activity together

Dear Parent or Carer

If necessary, please show your child how to tie their shoe laces.

National Curriculum reference: AT 1, AT 2 and AT 5

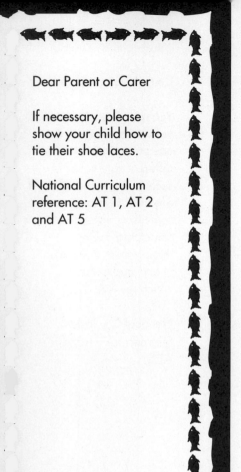

_____and

child

_____

helper(s)

_____

did this activity together

Shoelace tying competition

- Can you get faster at tying your shoelaces?

- Try it three times on Saturday and three times on Sunday.

- Make a chart to show your times.

- You may like to have a family competition and record all the times!

impact MATHS HOMEWORK

Making an ice cube

● How long does it take to make an ice cube?

I put water in the freezer at:

I think it will be frozen in

minutes.

My water had frozen at :

My water took

minutes to freeze.

Dear Parent or Carer

Your child may like to flavour some of the water with fruit juice. Does this alter the time taken for the liquid to freeze?

National Curriculum reference: AT 1, AT 2 and AT 5

_____and

child

_____

helper(s)

_____

did this activity together

impact MATHS HOMEWORK

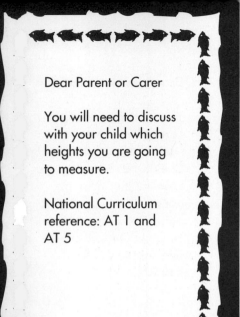

_____and

child

_____

helper(s)

_____

did this activity together

Take a seat

● Are all the chairs in your house the same height?

● Make a list of different things used for sitting on.

● Measure their heights.

● Please bring your lists to school.

impact MATHS HOMEWORK

How much milk do you drink in a week?

● Each time milk is delivered to your home or bought, record the quantity and type on the bottle shape below.

● Make a chart of your information and bring it to school.

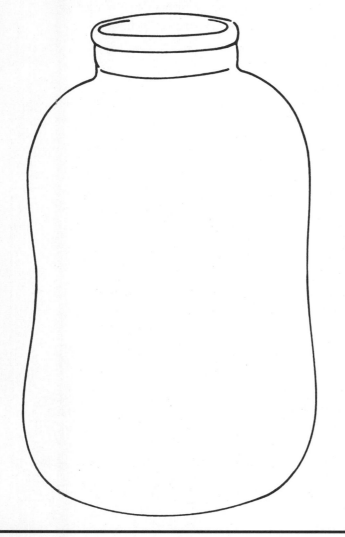

Dear Parent or Carer

Please encourage your child to think of a method of recording, he or she may need help with the construction of the chart.

National Curriculum reference: AT 1 and AT 5

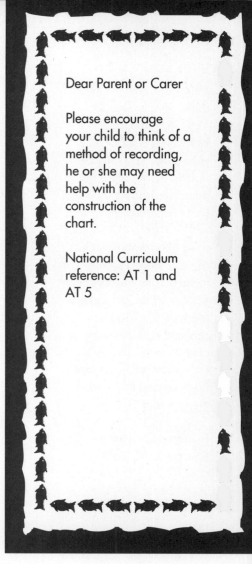

_____and

child

_____

helper(s)

_____

did this activity together

_____and

child

_____

helper(s)

_____

did this activity together

School, TV, sleep

YOU WILL NEED: three different coloured crayons or felt-tipped pens.

● Use the three colours to shade the times you spend at school, watching TV and sleeping. Use a different colour for each activity. Perhaps you could use a key to record how your colours have been used; for example, blue for sleeping.

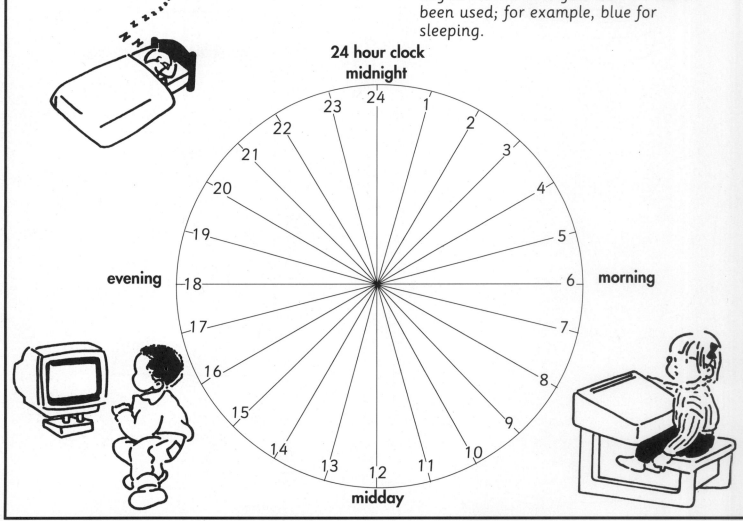

impact MATHS HOMEWORK

Screw-top survey

● How many lids at home have screw tops?

● How many turns does it take to remove the tops?

● Design a chart below to show the number of turns taken to remove the tops.

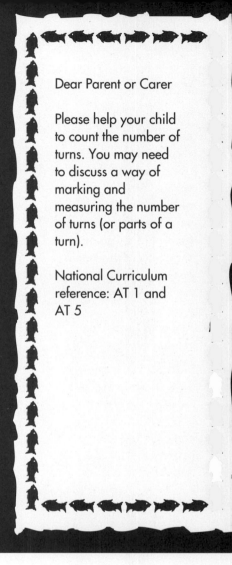

Dear Parent or Carer

Please help your child to count the number of turns. You may need to discuss a way of marking and measuring the number of turns (or parts of a turn).

National Curriculum reference: AT 1 and AT 5

_____and

child

_____

helper(s)

_____

did this activity together

_____and

child

_____

helper(s)

_____

did this activity together

How far to work?

● How far does each member of your family travel to work?

● Design a chart (you could use the back of this sheet) to show, for each family member:

• the distance travelled;

• how they travel;

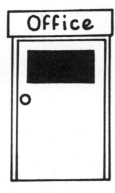

• where they travel to.

• the time taken.

● Bring your chart to school.

Holidays

● What was your best ever day out? Or where was your last holiday?

● How did you travel there?

● How long did it take to get there?

We left home at:

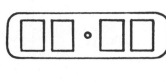

We arrived at:

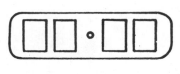

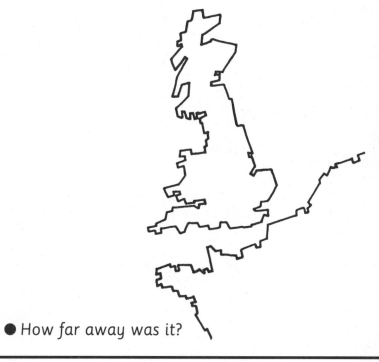

● How far away was it?

_____and

child

_____

helper(s)

_____

did this activity together

_____and

child

_____

helper(s)

_____

did this activity together

Cornflakes

● Design a chart to show the brands, packet sizes and costs of cornflakes. Start by using the space below.

● Please bring your information into school.

impact MATHS HOMEWORK

Milk prices

● Make a milk survey in the supermarket.

● What quantities is milk sold in?

● How many varieties are there?

● How much do they cost?

● If possible, please bring an empty milk carton into school along with your information.

_____and

child

_____

helper(s)

_____

did this activity together

_____and

child

_____

helper(s)

_____

did this activity together

Five minutes peace

● Can you be quiet for five whole minutes?

● Ask someone to time you.

● Draw in the times when you started and when you finished on these clocks.

● Draw a picture below of what you did while you were totally quiet!

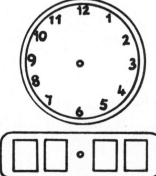

Colour chance

YOU WILL NEED: an old birthday or Christmas card, some crayons, a pencil and some counters (small bricks, coins or raisins will do).

● Cut out the spinner on this page.

● Mount it on to the back of an old birthday or Christmas card.

● Cut round it and colour two of the segments in red, two in green, two in blue and two in yellow.

● Stick a pencil through the middle.

● With your helper, choose from your spinner a 'plus' (+) colour and a 'minus' (–) colour each.

● Start with six counters each and put the rest in a pile in the middle.

● Take it in turns to spin the spinner. If it lands on your + colour, take a counter from the pile in the middle. If it lands on your – colour you must give a counter from your own pile to your partner. (If you have no counters left, do nothing!)

● Have six goes each. Who has the most counters?

● Play again. Does the same person win?

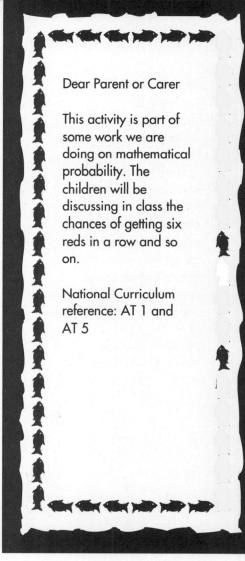

Dear Parent or Carer

This activity is part of some work we are doing on mathematical probability. The children will be discussing in class the chances of getting six reds in a row and so on.

National Curriculum reference: AT 1 and AT 5

_____and

child

_____

helper(s)

_____

did this activity together

Dear Parent or Carer

This game leads into some work which we are doing in class on probability. We shall be discussing the mathematical probability of certain outcomes occurring. Please help your child to record their scores carefully so that we can use them in class.

National Curriculum reference: AT 1 and AT 5

_____and

child

_____

helper(s)

_____

did this activity together

Lucky aces

YOU WILL NEED: the four aces from a pack of cards and a score sheet.

● Take it in turns to throw the cards gently in the air. How do they land?

● Score as follows:

0 points for any which land face down;
1 point for the ace of clubs (face up);
2 points for the ace of diamonds (face up);
3 points for the ace of hearts (face up);
4 points for the ace of spades (face up).

● Record all your scores each go. Play until someone has ten points.

● Bring your scores into school.

impact MATHS HOMEWORK

Lucky aces

Name	Throw number	Number of cards face down (0 points)	♣ Ace of clubs (1 point)	♦ Ace of diamonds (2 points)	♥ Ace of hearts (3 points)	♠ Ace of spades (4 points)	Total

Name	Throw number	Number of cards face down (0 points)	♣ Ace of clubs (1 point)	♦ Ace of diamonds (2 points)	♥ Ace of hearts (3 points)	♠ Ace of spades (4 points)	Total

impact MATHS HOMEWORK

Dear Parent or Carer

We are exploring mathematical probability at the moment and we shall be discussing the chances of a book opening at a particular page. Help your child to choose a book with not too many pages (about 25 is fine) – this will make our calculations easier!

National Curriculum reference: AT 1 and AT 5

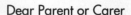

_____and

child

_____

helper(s)

_____

did this activity together

Open book

● Open one of your favourite books at random. What page does it land on? Let someone else open it. What page do they get?

● Try this at least ten times with as many people as you can. Record which page numbers you get.

● How many pages are there in the book?

● Bring all your figures back into class.

Chatterbox

● What are the chances of you talking for three minutes without using the words 'yes' or 'no'?!

● Try this out with as many people as you can! (You will need some way to time them for three minutes, such as a watch or clock.)

● Here's how. Say 'Start' and then ask them a question. They must reply and you then ask another question and so on. But, if they say either 'Yes' or 'No' they are 'out'!

● Then you have a turn with someone else asking the questions.

● Record all the tries. How many minutes do people manage?

● Bring your findings into school.

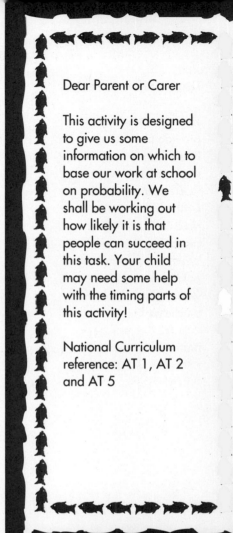

Dear Parent or Carer

This activity is designed to give us some information on which to base our work at school on probability. We shall be working out how likely it is that people can succeed in this task. Your child may need some help with the timing parts of this activity!

National Curriculum reference: AT 1, AT 2 and AT 5

_____and

child

_____

helper(s)

_____

did this activity together

_____and

child

_____

helper(s)

_____

did this activity together

Page view

● What are your chances of opening a book on a page without the word 'the' on it?

● Choose a picture book – one with only a line or a couple of lines of print on each page.

● Check each page. How many have the word 'the' on them? Write down the number of pages with the word 'the' and write down the number of pages without the word 'the'.

● Now ask someone to open the book at random ten times. Before they do this, both guess how many times he or she will open the book at a page with a 'the' on it.

● Record how many of the random openings actually do find a 'the' page.

● Was it more or less than you expected?

● Bring your work into school.

impact MATHS HOMEWORK

Head start

YOU WILL NEED: a coin.

● How likely is it that I will throw a coin and it will land as 'heads' four times in a row?

● Work with a partner so that one of you can spin the coin and the other can record how it lands.

● How many times do you have to spin it to get four heads in a row? Before you start, have a guess!

● Were you right? Bring the record of all your throws into class.

Dear Parent or Carer

This activity is designed to help your child explore the concept of mathematical probability. We shall discuss in school how many times we could reasonably expect to have to spin the coin in order to get four heads in a row. Of course, life does not always conform to mathematical expectations!

National Curriculum reference: AT 1 and AT 5

_____and
child

_____
helper(s)

_____

did this activity together

_____and

child

_____

helper(s)

_____

did this activity together

Letter chances

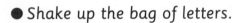

YOU WILL NEED: a bag containing ten small pieces of card with letters of the alphabet written on them.

● Shake up the bag of letters.

● Take a letter out of the bag. Don't show it to anyone else.

● Can your helper guess what letter it is? If they guess correctly, they must say a word beginning with that letter. If they can do this they keep the letter.

● If they guess incorrectly, you have to say a word beginning with that letter. If you can do this, you keep the letter.

● Now let your helper have a turn at taking a letter out of the bag.
If you can guess which letter they have picked and you can say a word beginning with that letter, you can keep the letter. If not, and they can say a word beginning with that letter, then they can keep the letter.

● Keep playing like this until the bag is empty! Who has the most letters?

impact MATHS HOMEWORK

Red winner

YOU WILL NEED: 12 small cards (made out of the back of an old birthday or Christmas card) with one coloured dot on each card: 6 red, 2 blue, 2 green, 1 yellow and 1 orange.

● Shuffle the cards and deal out six, face down, in front of each player.

● Take it in turns to turn over one of your six cards. Before you do so, you must say what colour you think it will be. If you are right, score as follows:

Red = 5 points;

Blue or green = 10 points;

Yellow or orange = 15 points.

● When all the cards have been turned over the person with the most points wins.

Dear Parent or Carer

This activity will help your child to come to understand the basic laws of probability. He or she will have consider the likelihood of certain events. You can help by getting her or him to think about whether the guesses are sensible!

National Curriculum reference: AT 1 and AT 5

_____and

child

_____

helper(s)

_____

did this activity together

Number chances

YOU WILL NEED: ten small pieces of card (the back of an old Christmas or birthday card will do fine) and a paper bag.

● Write the numbers 1–10 on the cards.

● Put the cards into the paper bag and shake them up.

● Now play this game. Take it in turns to close your eyes and remove one piece of card from the bag. If it is an odd number, keep it. If it is even, put it back into the bag. Keep playing until all the odd numbers have been taken.

● The person with the highest score is the winner.

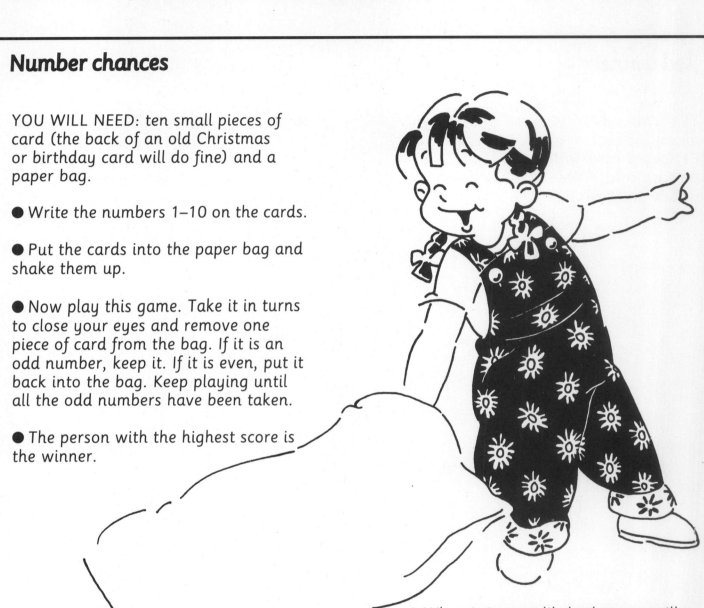

● When is it most likely that you will pull an odd number out of the bag?

● When is it least likely?

impact MATHS HOMEWORK

Coin sandwich

YOU WILL NEED: a coin.

● Take it in turns to toss the coin three times. Note down what you get each time like this:
HHT means head, head, tail;
HTT means head, tail, tail.

● Every time you get a 'coin sandwich' – either HTH or THT – score 10 points.

● The first person to get 50 points is the winner.

● Would it make the game easier or harder if you had to get HHH or TTT to get 10 points?
Try it and see!

Dear Parent or Carer

This game helps children to think about the relative likelihood of certain outcomes. Is it harder to get three heads than three tails? This develops ideas necessary for the study of probability.

National Curriculum reference: AT 1 and AT 5

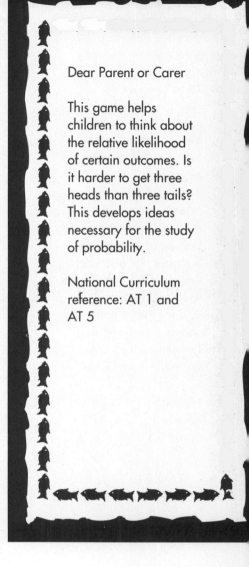

_____and

child

_____

helper(s)

_____

did this activity together

_____and
child

_____
helper(s)

_____

did this activity together

Card shuffle

YOU WILL NEED: ten small cards, numbered 1–10. (They could be made out of the back of an old birthday or Christmas card.)

● Shuffle the cards and put them in a pile face down.

● Take it in turns to take one off the top. Before you look at it, you are allowed to say two numbers that you think it might be.

● If it is one of those, keep the card. If not, put it back underneath the rest, face down.

● When all the cards have gone, the winner is the one with the most cards.

● Play several times. Do you get better at guessing?!

impact MATHS HOMEWORK

Spinning maths

YOU WILL NEED: three coloured crayons and a pencil.

● Cut out the spinner at the bottom of this page and colour it in. Choose three colours; colour two quarters in one colour and one quarter in each of the other two colours.

● Push a pencil through the middle of the spinner and spin it.

● Which colour does it land on?

● Spin it several times. Which colour does it mostly land on?

● Keep a record on the back of this sheet of your spins and the colours it lands on.

● Which colour do you think it is most likely to land on?

● Which colour do you think it is least likely to land on?

Dear Parent or Carer

This game helps children think about likelihood and how probable or improbable certain events are. They will also have to work hard at remembering which cards have gone!

National Curriculum reference: AT 1, AT 2 and AT 5

_____and

child

_____

helper(s)

_____

did this activity together

IMPACT diaries

The IMPACT diaries provide a mechanism by means of which an efficient parent-teacher dialogue is established. Through these diaries, which last up to two years depending upon the frequency of the IMPACT tasks, teachers obtain valuable feedback both about children's performances on specific maths tasks and about the tasks themselves. Parents are able to alert the teacher to weaknesses and strengths and nothing about the child's performance in maths comes as a big surprise at the end of the year or when the statutory assessments are administered. The diaries are a crucial part of this homework scheme.

Help with implementing IMPACT

Schools that wish to get IMPACT started by means of a series of staff meetings or in-service days may like to purchase the IMPACT INSET pack which contains everything that is needed for getting going. This is available from IMPACT Supplies Ltd, PO Box 1, Woodstock, Oxon OX20 1HB.

Useful telephone numbers

IMPACT Central Office (for information and assistance): 071 607 2789 at the University of North London on extension 6349.
IMPACT Supplies Ltd (for diaries and INSET pack): 0993 812895.

Correlation of the Scottish maths curriculum with the English curriculum

The Scottish curriculum is divided into the Attainment Outcomes given below.

(PSE) Problem-solving and enquiry skills

(IH) Information handling

(NMM) Number, money and measurement

(SPM) Shape, position and movement

PSE is the equivalent of the English AT 1

IH permeates the Scottish maths curriculum, in that its requirements apply to all maths activities in NMM and SPM.

English	Subject	Scottish
AT 2	Number	NMM
AT 2	Money	NMM
AT 2	Measuring	NMM
AT 3	Algebra	NMM
AT 4	Shape and space	SPM
AT 5	Data handling	IH

LEVELS

Scottish	English
A	1/2
B	2/3
C	3/4
D	4/5
E	5/6

Correlation of the Northern Ireland maths curriculum with the English curriculum

The Northern Ireland curriculum is divided into the Attainment Targets (ATs) given below.

(AT N) Number

(AT A) Algebra

(AT M) Measures

(AT S) Shape and space

(AT D) Handling data

English	Subject	Northern Ireland
AT 2	Number	AT N
AT 2	Money	AT M
AT 2	Measuring	AT M
AT 3	Algebra	AT A
AT 4	Shape and space	AT S
AT 5	Data handling	AT D

LEVELS

N Ireland	English
1/2	1/2
2/3	2/3
3/4	3/4
4/5	4/5
5/6	5/6

impact MATHS HOMEWORK